The Legend of
COMMANDARIA
3000 years of wine making tradition

Antonis Constantinou

Copyright © Antonis Constantinou
for the English language

Front page illustration
Antonis Constantinou

This book draws on pictures and material from
«ΡΗΓΑΔΕΣ ΙΠΠΟΤΕΣ ΡΑΓΙΑΔΕΣ...κρασί»
Copyright © Antonis Constantinou
Copyright © KEDROS Editions, Athens (for the Greek language)

The right of Antonis Constantinou to be acknowedged as the author of this work is protected by law. Copying or publication of this work, in whole or in part, in paper or by electronic means, is unlawful, unless with written permission of Antonis Constantinou.

ISBN: 9789464593822 (paperback)
ISBN: 9789464593839 (ebook)

To the memery of my parents Polycarpos and Polymnia and of all their contemporaries who laboured to keep the traditions of winemaking alive against unfavourable odds

TABLE OF CONTENTS

Chapter I:	Introducing the Legend of Commandaria	1
Chapter II:	Commandaria before it was called Commandaria	5
Chapter III:	The wine of Cyprus makes a triumphant entry into the Latin West	11
Chapter IV:	Commandaria becomes an important trade commodity	21
Chapter V:	14th century: the golden age of Commandaria	31
Chapter VI:	Fortified Commandaria and the *vinum maroali*: venturing into the latin vocabulary	61
Chapter VII:	Trade in Commandaria through the centuries	67
Chapter VIII:	The technology of Commandaria production	77
Chapter IX:	Commandaria in modern times	104

CHAPTER I

INTRODUCING THE LEGEND OF COMMANDARIA

What is Commandaria?

Wine lovers and wine historians will be delighted to know that there is a wine in the world, different from others and very distinct, whose history and methods of production go back unchanged over 3000 years. A wine that the ancients called "Nama" and in medieval times was known as "le vin de la Comandarie" or simply "Commandaria". During the first historically recorded wine competition organised by King Philip August of France in 1223, it was crowned 'Pope of the wines' and a century later, the Roman Pontifixes seated in Avignon preferred it to their Chateauneuf du Pape. Other learned men of the Catholic Church, such as St. Bernard and St. Thomas Aquinas, associated Commandaria with the "Botrus Cipri" mentioned in verse 14 of King Salomon's "Song of Songs". Saint Gregory even stated that it surpassed all the wines of the world, just as Salomon's love of wisdom surpassed that of the bride.

In the Eastern Church, Commandaria was used since early Christian times for the Holy Communion, representing Christ's blood. Constantius, Archbishop of Sinai, spoke of it in the 18th century as "the fragrant nectar of Zeus that flows abundantly from the holy temple of his beloved son Bacchus" whereas, a century earlier, travellers Porcacci and Cotovicus referred to Commandaria as a "balm" and attributed to it healing properties when consumed with moderation.

Today, Commandaria is a Protected Designation of Origin registered with the European Union like many others. From a historical point of view, however, it would not be an exaggeration to call it the most ancient denomination of origin in Europe, a wine that has always been produced in a well-defined geographical area using the same indigenous varieties of grapes and employing standardised methods that remained unchanged.

This booklet sketches the history of this legendary wine from ancient times to the present and attempts to substantiate this claim by making reference to relevant written records and authentic information. The booklet is also of value as a historical review text since the history of Commandaria was inextricably linked to the fortunes of its homeland, Cyprus, especially when it was a Frankish kingdom and the seat of the military crusader Orders of the Temple and the Hospital. It offers important insights into the history of Cyprus and the crusades that visitors of this beautiful Mediterranean country, also called the "island of Venus", will certainly appreciate and enjoy.

What kind of wine is Commandaria? What makes it different?

Commandaria is a sweet dessert wine with an alcoholic content typically in the order of 15%, mostly reached using natural methods of production and vinification. The addition of pure alcohol of grape origin is not excluded but is normally not required.

Other than the specific indigenous grape varieties it is produced from (a black one called "Mavro" and a white one called

"Xynisteri") and the sun-drenched areas where they are grown, what makes Commandaria different from other wines is the way the grapes are treated before the juice is extracted to start vinification. The method was first described by *Hesiod* around 700 BC in his book "Works and Days".

The grapes are collected well-matured, usually after the 15th of September, and are first laid out in the sun for ten to twenty days to lose water. Extracting the juice from the semi-dry grapes is done using special equipment and, in pre-industrial times, this led to the development of heavy-duty wooden presses that will be described further down. Only the grape juice and the suspensions it contains are used for further vinification. The rest is being discarded and typically used to produce a powerful spirit called "zivania".

Traditionally, vinification was done at normal temperatures and the producers relied on natural processes to stop the alcoholic fermentation without excluding the use of other means. Typically, the wine requires ageing to reach its full potential and the longer it is kept, the better its quality. In the past, the wine started off having a deep red colour, but, with time, it developed a yellowish appearance as the suspensions or sediments settled to the ground. The layer formed in this way at the bottom of the containers was called the 'mother of the wine' and was never removed, not even during transport, because it was thought to be the principal source of the wine's full body and round taste. Nowadays, the colour is more standardized.

A detailed description of the ageing and change of colour of Commandaria in past centuries is found in the books of Stefano de Lusignan from the sixteenth century and of Giovanni Mariti from the eighteenth century. Stefano de Lusignan, a scion of the Frankish royal family of Cyprus, referred to Commandaria in

1573 AD as a "*delicious, refined, and strong wine that speaks to the heart. When still fresh, it has a dark colour and is sweet as honey. Then it slowly loses its dark colour and sweetness and acquires a pleasant smell. As it ages, it turns whiter, smells sweet, and becomes perfect. If you don't tamper with it, the wine can hold until the barrel rots. In fact, some of our nobles have wines that are sixty and eighty years old. And every year they use them only to help the sick. If you remove 5 or 6 parts from the barrel and fill it with good fresh wine during the new harvest, the old wine will never spoil. It can even be used as a balm.*"

Giovanni Mariti, a Correspondent Member of the Academy of Agricultural Experts of Florence, who was an official of the consulate of the Emperor of Tuscany in Ottoman Cyprus, wrote in 1769 that "*when Commandaria is fresh it has a rich red colour like Chianti. After a year, it starts losing its red colour and tends towards yellow, and the older it is, the more pleasant it becomes so that 8 or 10-years-old wine resembles in colour our muscadine. During the change, the suspensions (which in Cyprus are called the mother of the wine) settle in large quantities. These give 'body' to the wine and are never removed except to be transferred from one jar to another*".

Mariti also informs us that the practice of leaving the wine to age for many years was widely applied for a very special reason. "*It is customary,*" he wrote, "*when a child is born, for his father to put a well-sealed jar of wine in the ground, where it stays until the child's wedding day when it is served during the wedding celebration and distributed to relatives and friends. This wine can be 20 or more years old. It is never sold but kept and offered as a gift to the wedding guests. On the market, the oldest wine you can find is 8 to 10 years old.*"

CHAPTER II

COMMANDARIA BEFORE IT WAS CALLED COMMANDARIA

A wine produced since time immemorial

As mentioned earlier, the name Commandaria comes from the medieval French "vin de la Comandarie', which was used to describe the wine produced and exported by the Knights of St. John from about the end of the thirteenth century AD onwards. It is via the mercantile and transport activities of this religious Order that the sweet wine of Cyprus became known all over Europe under the name Commandaria. We will discuss the role of the Knights of St. John in producing and exporting wine and other goods from Cyprus in more detail later.

Before 1300 AD, Commandaria was simply known as the "wine of Cyprus" and it is under this name that it won the first prize at the wine contest in Paris in 1223 AD, mentioned before. Its production can be traced back several thousand years before our time. We don't know exactly how far back, but there is evidence that wine was traded at least as early as 2300 years BC, the dating of a shipwreck discovered in 1999 near the shores of Cyprus which carried over 2500 amphorae used for the transport of wine. In 2005, the chemical signatures of 18 round earthen flasks stored in the Cyprus Museum in Nicosia and dating from the Chalcolithic or copper-stone period (3500-3000 BC) were examined by a team of Italian archaeologists led by Maria-Rosaria Belgiorno. In twelve of them, they identified traces of tartaric acid (a component of wine), proving that they were used for the storage of wine. The flasks were first unearthed between 1932 and 1935 during excavations on the outskirts of the village of Erimi, near Limassol, headed by the late Porphyrios Dikaios, then curator of the Cyprus Museum.

Starting in about the twelfth century BC, several Greek colonies were founded on Cyprus. Soon, the Greek culture of antiquity spread to the island as well. Homer, the author of *Iliad* and the *Odyssey,* thought to have lived in the ninth century BC, informs us that the wine of Cyprus was widely known in his time and was referred to as the "sweet wine of Cyprus". He also informs us that the Mycenaeans of mainland Greece invited the Greek cities of Cyprus to join in the war against Troy. Kinyras, the king of Paphos, sent a sizable fleet that took part in the hostilities.

Supplying an army with enough wine was quite important in classical times and continued to be so until the late Middle Ages. For the combatants who engaged in those terrible man-to-man fights, sword and shield at hand, the stirring effect of a potent wine like Commandaria must have been equal to natural adrenaline in the struggle for survival and victory.

Evidently, Cyprus was producing enormous quantities of wine in those days, and they found their way to many other parts of the Greek world. The Athenian tragedian *Euripides*, writing in the fifth century BC, referred to the wine of Cyprus as "Nama", a word that literally means flowing abundantly, like a stream. Gradually however, "Nama" also came to signify a source of inspiration and, figuratively, a drink that has the qualities of nectar, the drink of the ancient Gods. As mentioned earlier, *Hesiod*, another classical author, described the basic technique employed in producing a potent sweet wine like Commandaria around 700 BC.

Cyprus was considered by the ancient Greeks to be the birthplace of Aphrodite or Venus, the Goddess of Love, and it is here that the main Shrine and Holy Gardens of the Goddess and her beloved Adonis were located. The cult of Dionysus or Bacchus, the God of Wine, was also widespread and even today certain locations in the valley of the river Kouris, traditionally the heart of the island's winegrowing region, continue to bear the name Dionysus.

As expected, depictions showing winemaking and drinking practices were very common on wine amphorae and other pots from classical times. An entire collection of them was presented by Karageorgis in a specialist publication.[1] The same applied to various types of mosaics, notably on floors. The most famous are the ones from a Roman villa in Paphos dating from the second century AD. Paphos was the capital of Cyprus during the Roman period and this villa probably belonged to a high-ranking administration official. Dionysus, the Greek God of wine, dominates the themes of the impressive, well-preserved mosaics in rich and beautiful colours, covering the villa's 559 square meters of floors.

---

[1] Vassos Karageorghis, *Aspects of Everyday Life in Ancient Cyprus. Iconographic Representations*, Nicosia, A.G. Leventis Foundation, 2006, pp. 6-14.

A section of the floor of the "Villa of Dionysus" in Paphos, Cyprus. Dionysus and Agme are shown on the left, king Ikarus carrying a load of wine in the middle, and the "first wine drinkers" in a merry condition on the right.

The villa's mosaics depict mythological scenes such as "The Triumph of Dionysus", "Dionysus and Akme", "Icarus and the shepherds", "Icarus and Dionysus", as well as scenes of loving couples: "Phaedra and Hippolytus", "Pyramus and Thisbe", "Poseidon and Amymone".[2]

The cult of Dionysus involved taking part in religious mysteries and secret rituals, the details of which are not fully understood by historians. They comprised entering a state of religious trance by consuming liberal quantities of wine, indulging for hours in a kind of erotic dance. The male believers were called *satyrs* and the female *maenads*.

According to the Italian novelist and scholar Massimo

---

[2] Demetrios Michaelides, *Cypriot Mosaics*, Nicosia, Department of Antiquities, 1992 (Second edition), pp. 27-37·

Manfredi, who wrote the famous trilogy "Alexander the Great", Olympias, the Macedonian conqueror's mother, was a devoted follower of Bacchus and she often took part in the Dionysian mysteries. Alexander himself was a big lover of wine. Being an archaeologist, Manfredi knew very well that the sweet wine of Cyprus was famous at the time of this great king. Therefore, in his novelised description of Alexander's campaigns, he wants the wine of Cyprus to flow abundantly during the frequent banquets the Macedonian king was holding to celebrate his victories on the way from Greece to the Hindus River. During one of those feasts, fully intoxicated and out of control, Alexander slayed Philotas, the son of his general Parmenion, for alleged disloyalty.

After the Christianization of the Roman Empire and the beginning of a new era in the East that came to be known as Byzantine, the Dionysian mysteries were branded as sinful orgies. Nevertheless, the sweet wine of Cyprus continued to be highly appreciated, and the Church found a role for it in the mystery of the Eucharist. In the Eastern Church, Commandaria has been used ever since to represent the Savior's blood in the Holy Communion. And the old traditions associated with the pagan gods resurfaced once the Renaissance freed Europe from the religious excesses of the Dark Ages. We have already quoted the poetic way in which Constantius, Archbishop of Sinai, described Commandaria in the 18th century.[3]

He was not the only Christian dignitary who referred to Commandaria using classical and biblical quotations. Stefano de Lusignan,[4] the sixteen-century historian and Doctor of Theology,

---

[3] Constantius was in Cyprus in 1776 but his book was published in 1819.
[4] Stefano Lusignano di Cipro, *Chorograffia et breve historia universale dell' isola de Cipro...*, Bologna, 1573, (translated into English by Olimpia Pelosi, State University of New York, 2001), p. 85

informs us that learned Catholic dignitaries like St. Bernard and St. Thomas Aquinas believed that King Salomon carried vine root stock from Cyprus to plant his vineyard in Engadin. They inferred this from verse 14 of chapter 1 of the Song of Songs: *"Botrus Cipri dilectus meus mihi in vinis Engadin"*. In loose translation of the original Greek text, it speaks of *"My beloved one who is to me like a bunch of Cypriot grapes in the vineyards of Engadin."*

Another medieval traveller, the German Rudolf von Südheim, writing in 1340 AD, even insisted that the vineyards of Engadin were in Cyprus itself. When he had stopped on the island a few years earlier, he visited a large vineyard in the village of Phinikas near Paphos that extended beyond the reach of the eye.[5] He saw another one in Colos near Limassol, almost as big as the one in Paphos, and decided that these must be the ones referred to in the Bible as the vineyards of Engadin.

---

[5] Claude Delaval Cobham, *Excerpta Cypria*, Cambridge, 1908, p. 19, 22

CHAPTER III

THE WINE OF CYPRUS MAKES A TRIUMPHANT ENTRY INTO THE LATIN WEST

A brief review of the history of the religious Orders of the Temple and St. John and their role in the Frankish kingdom of Cyprus

Until the end of the 12th century, Cyprus was part of the Byzantine Empire. Starting in 1192 AD, it became a Latin kingdom and, from then onwards, the history of its wine was inextricably linked with the Frankish rule and with the religious military Orders of the Knights Templar and St. John who settled in Cyprus shortly thereafter. It was a glorious period for the sweet wine of Cyprus that changed name along the way, as we will see further down. But, before we do so, it is perhaps important to present shortly the historical context of the period.

Following the success of the first crusade and the capture of Jerusalem in 1099, a Christian kingdom and several principalities and counties were established in the Middle East and the Holy Land. Most of them were short-lived because of the rise of a formidable enemy in the region to whom the Christians were no match. A Muslim leader of Kurdish descent, in the West known as Saladin, established himself in Egypt in 1169 AD and, a few years later, moved against the Christian dominions. In 1187, he lured the army of Guy de Lusignan, the inexperienced new king of Jerusalem, into a desert region near Tiberias and destroyed it. Within a few months, Jerusalem and all Christian cities to the south of Tyre in today's Lebanon fell into his hands. Starting in 1190, fresh Christian armies arriving from Europe regained most of the coastal cities but failed to recapture Jerusalem. The chief leader of the third crusade, the King of England Richard the Lionheart, signed a peace treaty with Saladin and, in 1192, returned to Europe. The presence of the Latin Christians in the Holy Land was thus extended until 1292 AD, when their last stronghold in Syria, the castle of St. John of Acre, fell into the hands of the Mamluks of Egypt.

Until 1190 AD, the island of Cyprus was part of the Byzantine Empire, and was then captured by Richard the Lionheart on his way to the Holy Land. After a short-lived transfer to the Knights Templar, the island was sold to Guy de Lusignan, the defeated former king of Jerusalem. Guy and his brother and successor Amalric established in Cyprus a Frankish kingdom ruled by the Lusignan dynasty until 1489 AD when the island came under the control of Venice. In 1570/71, an Ottoman army under Lala Mustafa Pasha conquered Cyprus and thus ended the so-called Frankish period in the island's history.

During the 13th and most of the 14th century, the kingdom of Cyprus was quite strong and carried the crusader spirit fort. At the height of its power, King Peter I (1359-1369) subjugated the Turkish Emirs in southern Asia Minor and in 1365 captured Alexandria in Egypt but could not hold it for more than three days. Soon after, a Genoese intervention into the kingdom's internal affairs initiated a period of decline. Following the battle of Khirokitia in 1426 AD, Cyprus became a vassal kingdom, paying an annual tribute to the Mamluk Sultanate of Egypt.

In the early years of the kingdom's life, many Christian nobles and other refugees from the Middle East settled in Cyprus at the invitation of Guy de Lusignan to "latinize" the island. The feudal system replaced the Byzantine land tenure and the assizes,[6] the unwritten laws of the kingdom of Jerusalem, were applied in Cyprus too. The Frankish immigrants were divided into nobles and burgesses. Fiefs in various parts of Cyprus were given to the nobles depending on their status but they mostly lived in Nicosia making up the king's court. The burgesses comprised artisans and scribes and their affairs were judged by a separate court called "cour de bourgeois". They also lived in the cities, notably in Famagusta. There were also a few Latins, mostly of Syrian origin, who lived in the countryside and worked for the local lords. From a church point of view, they were grouped into "priories" and were served by catholic priests commonly called "priors". Stefano de Lusignan mentions six such priories.

For the Greek Orthodox people of Cyprus, the Frankish period was a very difficult one. Under the feudal system, they were deprived of their properties and, with minor exceptions, were reduced to the lowest social class of paroikoi. Under the assizes, the paroikoi were treated like slaves who belonged to their feudal lord and did not have the right to move to another property unless exchanged with someone else in mutual agreement between their respective masters. They could not be owners of

---

[6] From the Latin term assisiae, which meant the sessions of the court, its decisions and the law on the basis of which they were issued. The assises were a collection of laws formulated in medieval French, originally enacted for the kingdom of Jerusalem and later for the kingdom of Cyprus, defining the rights and obligations of the nobility and bourgeoisie. They were based on oral tradition and were recorded according to the legislation of the 12th and 13th centuries. The texts were collected by Philip of Novara and his student, the great jurist John d'Ibelin (Livre de Jean d'Ibelin, 1265-1266).

land unless they became freemen by paying a sizable amount of money or, more usually, because their master had decided so for his own reasons. Even then, they paid heavy taxes in kind and had to contribute part of their labour to the local feudal lord. The cost of labour was thus minimised, and this favoured the expansion of agricultural activities, in particular the production of wine, which was in strong demand and fetched a good price.

The Catholic Church and the members of several religious Orders, who settled in Cyprus soon after it had become a Latin kingdom, also played an important role in the island's history. Foremost among them were the two military Orders of knighted monks known as the Templars and the Hospitallers or Knights of St. John of Jerusalem. During the previous century, they had been spearheading the crusader armies, manning the border fortresses and helping to defend the Christian possessions in the Holy Land. At the beginning of the 13th century, King Hugh I of Cyprus granted to them extensive properties in Cyprus to gain their favour, which he considered imperative for the survival of a Latin kingdom in the Middle East. When the last Christian stronghold fell in the hands of the Mamluks in 1292 AD, both Orders transferred their headquarters to Cyprus.

The Order of the Knights Templar, or "The Poor Companions of Christ and of the Temple of Jerusalem", as their official name went, had been founded in Jerusalem by 8 monks in 1118 AD and within 100 years it became a huge military and financial organization that owned properties all over Europe. They are credited for having established the first pan-European money transfer system for travellers. When the Holy Land seemed to have been lost to Western Christianity, the Order's influence went down drastically, and many European sovereigns started having second thoughts about the role of a religious army that only the pope could control. First among them was King Philip IV of France, who needed money for his endless wars and had been eyeing the Order's fortune for some time now. Under pressure from Philip, Pope Clement V, then based in Avignon in southern France, accused the Templars of heresy in 1307 and in 1312 dissolved the Order "for the good of the church", as he said. The following year, Philip of France burned at the stake the Grand Master of the Order John de Molay and two other regional Grand Masters. Most other Templars were persecuted and killed or jailed. The properties of their Order throughout Europe were confiscated and placed in the hands of their competitors, the Knights of the Hospital, who undertook to pay Philip of France a handsome amount of money as compensation "for his efforts to unveil the dangerous Templar heretics".

The Hospitallers took their name from the hostels they were running in the Holy City. Such a hostel was first established in 623 AD by the Italian merchants of the Amalfi region to offer shelter and care to the Christian pilgrims of the Holy Land. When Jerusalem was taken over by the Crusaders in 1099, the Order of the Hospital became a knightly military Order by a bull of Pope Paschal II in 1113. In the decades that followed, they played an instrumental role in the defence of the Holy Land and in offering care to the thousands of pilgrims now streaming to Jerusalem from all over Europe.

In Cyprus, the Hospitallers established themselves very well from the early 13th century on. Later, they acquired great wealth by inheriting the properties hitherto belonging to the Knights Templar. Shortly after 1312, the Order of the Hospital came to own 53 villages and rural settlements in Cyprus. Seven of these villages were in the fertile lowlands to the west of Limassol and around the Delta of the Kouris river, and 31 were upland villages in the eastern part of today's Limassol district, all together making up the Grand Commandery of the Colos. There was also the Small Commandery of Phinikas-Anogyra further to the west with five villages and the even smaller Commandery of Templos in Kyrenia.

In 1309 AD, the Order gained control over Rhodes and established a sovereign state with a large commercial fleet and a strong naval presence in the Eastern Mediterranean. From Rhodes, the Grand Master managed the Order's properties, domains and estates all over Europe by appointing commanders to look after them. The properties were therefore called commanderies, and their managers undertook to pay an annual "responsion" to the Order's treasury. The Hospitallers remained in Rhodes for 214 years before they were forced by the Turks to transfer their seat to Malta until 1798 and from there to Rome. They went down in history with many names: Hospitallers, Knights of St. John, Knights of Rhodes, Knights of Malta, and then again Knights of St. John until the present day.

The wine of Cyprus makes a triumphant entry into the Latin West

When the Franks arrived in Cyprus, they became aware of the potential income they could have from expanding the production of the island's excellent wine that was already held in great esteem both locally and abroad. This was confirmed soon after, when King Philip August of France (1180-1223 AD) organized a famous competition of white wines shortly before he died. The contest was described in a medieval poem by the French troubadour Henri d'Andeli entitled "*La bataillle des vins*" (the battle of wines)[7].

LA BATAILLE DES VINS

olez oïr une grant fable
Qu'il avint l'autrier fus la table
Au bon roi qui ot non Phelippe,
Qui volentiers moilloit fa pipe
1   Du bon vin qui eftoit du blanc.
Il le fenti gentil & franc,
Si le clamoit fon ameor.
Por le bien & por la douçor
Que li vins avoit dedenz foi,
10   Li rois en but fanz avoir foi.
Li rois qui eft cortois & fages
Manda a treftoz fes meffages
Qu'il alaiffent le meillor querre
Qu'il trovaiffent en nule terre.

In those times, white wines were very popular among the nobles of France, and this explains why King Philip August

---

[7] Henri d'Andeli, *La Bataille des Vins,* in Œuvres d'Henri d'Andeli, Rouen, 1880

organized a contest for white rather than red wines. The participation of the wine of Cyprus (vin de Chypre) meant that it was already well known in French circles who now viewed Cyprus as a kind of French "outre-mer" dominion. Various sources from that period inform us that the typical wine produced in Cyprus (the one that later came to be called Commandaria) started off as red but, with time, assumed a yellowish colour because its non-liquid suspensions settled to the bottom of the containers.

As Henri d'Andéli relates, at the beginning of the contest, the various wines were presented to the king in some sort of parade, starting with the wine of Cyprus. *Défilé des Vins: D'abord manda le vin de Chypre* (Parade of the wines: First started the wine of Cyprus).

King Philip tasted them and at the end he gave to each one a title. *Arrét du Roi: Le Roi couronna les bons vins. A chacun il donna un titre. Du vin de Chypre il fit un Pape qui resplendit comme une étoile. Il fit Cardinal e Légat le si gentil vin d'Aquilat.* (Ruling of the King: The king crowned the good wines. To each one he gave a title. Of the wine of Cyprus, he made a Pope, who shines like a star. Of the so fine wine of Aquilat, he made a Cardinal and Legate).

It should be noted that, in medieval times, the Pope was considered the supreme authority in the world, having the power to speak in the name of God and to legitimize or not a ruler's claim to sovereignty over a certain territory. He clearly stood above the kings and emperors, and commanded respect from all the Christian rulers of Western Europe.

Calling a wine "the Pope" meant that it was supreme and standing high above all other wines. A "Cardinal or Legate" was clearly subordinate and inferior to the Pope.

The designation "vin de Chypre" used by Henri d'Andeli

shows that the name Commandaria was not yet adopted during the first quarter of the 13th century. Although the Order of the Temple and that of the Hospital were both granted extensive estates in Cyprus by King Hugh I around 1210 AD, it was too soon for them to play an important role regarding winemaking and selling on the territory of the young kingdom.

The feudal system of land tenure favours the expansion of wine production

The feudal system introduced in Cyprus by Guy de Lusignan contributed considerably to the expansion of wine production in the 13th century for various reasons. First, because of the financial greediness of the nobles whom the king had granted many of the previous Byzantine estates. Having lost their properties in Syria, these nobles depended entirely on the income from their newly acquired estates in Cyprus for their subsistence. Wine was in great demand, and it was natural that they would try to maximize the revenue of their estates by planting new vines, increasing production as much as possible.

Second, because labour was abundant and cost almost nothing, given that the inhabitants of the villages were now turned into serfs and, even when they were allocated some land for their own use, they paid heavy taxes in kind and had to work without compensation for their lords at least two days per week.

Third, because the size of the holdings was now much bigger, and this allowed for economies of scale and for using an improved type of press that increased the efficiency of pressing and the yield of juice that could be extracted from grapes left in the sun to dry for 10-20 days. It is likely that the heavy wooden presses, that one can see today in rural museums of Cyprus and even *in situ,* were widely used in those times, exactly as they were in metropolitan France from the 12th century onwards.

The expansion of wine production was fostered, above all, by the increase in demand to cover the needs of the new aristocracy living in the cities and those of the crusader armies that continued to fight various wars in and around the Holy Land. Wine was consumed in large quantities, especially during periods of hostility, when it was used to incite the combatants before every battle. Joinville, a close adviser to King Louis IX of France, leader of the fifth crusade against Mamluk Egypt in 1249 AD, reports in his Chronicle that the officers of the king arrived in Limassol two years earlier and gathered vast quantities of cereals and wine for the needs of his expedition. Huge barrels of wine, he says, were stacked in the fields near the seashore.[8]

The availability of wine sometimes decided the outcome of a battle as several chroniclers of the siege of Famagusta by the Turks in 1570/71 passingly described. When the wine run out, they record, the fate of the city was finally decided after 12 months of siege.

---

[8] Cited by Nicholas Coureas in *Limassol from 1191 to 1300: Its Importance in the Context of Crusade, Trade and Settlement,* Crusades Subsidia 15, 2021

CHAPTER IV

COMMANDARIA BECOMES AN IMPORTANT TRADE COMMODITY

The role of the Knights of St. John (Hospitallers)

As mentioned earlier, both the Knights Templar and the Knights of St. John transferred their headquarters to Cyprus after losing Acre in 1292 AD. By then, both Orders owned extensive estates in Cyprus and the Order of St. John gained possession of all of them in 1312/13, when the Temple was dissolved by Pope Clement V. From the recording of the properties formerly belonging to the Temple and additional information published later by the chronicler Florios Voustronios, we learn that, soon after 1313, the Knights of St. John owned 53 villages.[9] In an-

---

[9] The list is presented by De Mas Latrie, *Histoire de l'île de Chypre*, Vol. 2, Paris, 1837, p. 109-110.

other document preserved by De Mas Latrie, dating from the beginning of the 16th century, the Hospitallers are shown to own 42 villages.[10] Combining the two lists, we conclude that the following properties belonged for shorter or longer periods to the Order of the Hospital (unknown villages are marked with an asterisk):

- 2 villages in the Paphos district (Inia, Akoursos);
- 5 villages between Limassol and Paphos (Phinikas, Anogyra, Agia Irini, Plataniskia, Caloyannata*), grouped together into the so-called Small Commandery of Phinikas-Anogyra;
- 38 villages grouped together into the so-called Grand Commandery of Colos, which comprised:
  - 7 villages in the fertile lowlands to the west of Limassol and around the Delta of the river Kouris (Colos, Erimi, Asomatos, Trachoni, Fasouri, Paramali and Sanatzia);
  - at least 31 villages and settlements in the hilly eastern part of today's Limassol district reaching up to the Troodos mountain range (Louvaras, Panagia of Louvaras, Villa, Agios Konstantinos, Agios Pavlos, Dierona, Sykopetra, Vigla, Sanida, Arakapas, Kellaki, Eftagonia, Klonari, Vasa, Monagrouli, Germasogeia, Mathikoloni, Agroades*, Armenochori, Paramytha, Apsiou, Gerasa, St. Rois (Riginos)*, Marameno, Mesorini*, Agios Georgios*, Agia Irini, Chira*, Livichi*, Andruclioti*, Iratovi* and other settlements in these areas);

---

[10] De Mas Latrie, *Histoire de l'île de Chypre*, 3, Paris, 1852, pp. 502-503

- 9 villages in the hilly areas to the south of the capital Nicosia (Akhera, Mitsero, Agrokipia, Mavrovouno, Kato Moni, Pardi*, Palaichori, Maroullena*, Kampi);
- 2 villages in the dry plain between Nicosia and Famagusta (Mora* and Angastina) and 2 in the Karpasia peninsula (Gastria and Kamares*);
- the village of Templos near Kyrenia (also referred to as the commandery of Templos);
- 3 villages in the Viscounty south of Nicosia (Psimolofou, which in 1321 went over to the Latin Patriarchate of Jerusalem, Kato Deftera and Trypi*);

Initially, the seat of the Knights of St. John was in Limassol. A small castle about 14 km to the west of Limassol was probably first built shortly after 1210 AD when King Hugh I of Cyprus granted the fertile lands around the village of Colos to the Hospital. In 1306 the castle went over to the Templars but returned to the Knights of St. John in 1313, together with many other Templar estates. The present castle in this place (see picture) was built in 1454 AD by the Grand Commander Louis de Magnac, whose coat-of-arms along with that of the Lusignan dynasty of Cyprus can be seen on the castle's walls.

The coat-of-arms of the Lusignan dynasty on the castle of Colos's wall.

In the rectangular courtyard (bailie) of the castle, the Hospitallers constructed a large sugar cane mill powered by the waters of the river Kouris that arrived there via a stone-built aqueduct.

The castle of Colos as it stands today. On the right, the remains of the sugar mill and aqueduct.

Today the castle of Colos and the remains of these facilities are open to the public and attract many visitors and tourists having an interest in medieval history and pre-industrial processing technology.

It would appear that the Knights of St. John, having lost their main role as defenders of the Holy Land and facilitators of the pilgrimage to the Savior's tomb following the loss of Acre in 1292 AD, were in search for new activities and sources of income to make themselves independent of transfers and religiously motivated donations from Europe. Cyprus offered them the possibility to develop new commercial activities by selling abroad agricultural commodities such as wine, cereals and sugar, to name only a few, that they produced in their own estates or could purchase from others.

On the 1st of November 1300 AD, the Grand Chapter of the Order met in Cyprus under the Grand Master Guillaume de Villaret and prepared a new constitution. Article 5 of the text regulates the sourcing and disposal of agricultural products in Cyprus and speaks for the first time about selling the surpluses of wine outside the Order.[11] [12]

> Art. 5. Establi est que tout le blé de la baillie de Chipre et de la comandarie de Limeson et le vin, salve la garnison acostumée de la baillye, veigne au granier et au selier, c'est à savoir : le blé et les leus [3] les aient assenez par tout Octobre au comandour de Limeson pour la despence dou covent, et le vin par tot Novenbre, salve le vin dou Quilane [4] qui fera à garder. Et quant le comandour de Chipre le voudra vendre, que le comandour de Limeson le puisse avoir pour tant come il en poroit avoir en la terre.

In loose translation, Article 5 determines that *"all the wheat of the bailie of Cyprus and the Commandery of Limassol and the wine, save* (the quantities needed to meet the needs of) *the garrison of the bailie, would be brought to the stores and cellars,*

---

[11] De Mas Latrie, *Histoire de l'île de Chypre*, 2, Paris, 1837, p. 90

[12] In the original text of Article 5, there was no reference to Quilane but to Quillac, possibly today's Kellaki, a village of the Grand Commandery of Colos. De Mas Latrie, interpreted Quillac as Quilane, today's Kilani (see further explanations in the text).

as follows: the wheat and the wine collected during October to the Commandery of Limassol for use by the Order; and so the wine of all November, save the wine of Quillac which will be kept. And when the Commander of Cyprus would like to sell it, the Commander of Limassol could have as much as he could get from the land."

Though very short, this text contains a wealth of information about the wine of Cyprus and the relevant activities of the Order of St. John. First, the Commander of Cyprus was officially authorized to engage in the sale of wine not only produced in the estates of the commandery of Limassol but also elsewhere, adding another lucrative business to the commercial activities of the Hospitallers. In the 14th century, the Knights of St. John were in fact engaged in the trade of quite a number of agricultural products from Cyprus. Other than wine, sugar and molasses, they exported several other commodities including cereals, pulses, almonds and carobs.[13]

The text of Article 5 also tells us that the Hospitallers were not only engaged in the collection and sale of cereals and wine produced in their own Commandery but also in the areas directly controlled by the Crown and other nobles of Cyprus. That is what the reference to the *baillie de Chypre* seems to imply. Similarly, the expression *salve la garnison acostumée de la bailye* is understood to refer to the surpluses remaining after the needs of the nobles and knights engaged in the defence of the kingdom had been satisfied. This shows that the Hospitallers deliberately made the choice to engage in "buying and selling"

---

[13] Nicolas Coureas, *Hospitaller Estates and Agricultural Production in Fourteenth and Fifteenth Century Cyprus*, in Emanuel Buttigieg & Simon Phillips (ed.), *Islands and Military Orders, c. 129-c.1798*, UK, Ashgate Publishing, 2013.

and, henceforth, they understood themselves as traders of agricultural products too. In Rhodes, where they had transferred their seat in 1309, they acquired a large fleet that they used for military and naval operations in times of war and for mercantile activities in times of peace.

Finally, Article 5 lets us conclude that the demand for wine exceeded the supply. Only the production potential of the land put a limit to the quantities available for sale. The Commander of Limassol was authorized to sell as much as the soil could give. The only exception was the wine of Quillac that had to be kept.

As mentioned above, De Mas Latrie, the French historiographer of the 19th century, interpreted Quillac as Quilane, today's Kilani, which was a famous royal domain producing, as it did in the 19th century and also today, a wine of excellent quality. De Mas Latrie certainly knew that Quilane did not belong to the Grand Commandery of Colos. By referring to it, he implicitly gave the same interpretation to Article 5 of the Hospitaller constitution of 1300 as we did, namely that they were not only trading their own wine but also any surpluses produced in other fiefs in the kingdom of Cyprus. In the next chapter, we will provide an explanation for the special treatment accorded to the wine produced in the village of Quilane which was probably required to meet the needs of the royal family. In medieval times, Quilane was a royal domain yielding a very rich income to the kings of Cyprus.

Whatever the case, it is at this period, i.e. the end of the 13th and the beginning of the 14th century, that the wine of Cyprus became known in many European countries as the "vin de la Commanderie", the wine of the Commandery of Cyprus, since it was traded by the Knights of St. John and was produced, at least the biggest part of it, in their Grand Commandery of Colos. This is the origin of the name Commandaria, a word deriving from Comandarie in medieval French (see the text of Article 5 of the constitution of the Order of St. John reproduced above).

A wine denomination was thus born, perhaps the very first in Europe, which was based on a well-defined geographical delimitation (indication in today's EU language), and a set of oenological specifications and production techniques that looked back to a tradition of over 2000 years. They would remain unchanged to the present day. Equally, an export commodity was born that would continue yielding sizeable profits and a rich income to all those who controlled its production and trade for the next five to six centuries.

As mentioned before, wine was not the only export commodity of the Hospitallers. They also exported sugar and molasses, cereals, almonds, carobs, cotton, and many other agricultural products from their estates in Cyprus. The nearby town of Limassol became the principal port of this trade. Nowadays a thriving tourist and financial centre, Limassol was known for centuries as just a place associated with the production and trade of wine. Over the centuries, various travellers returning to Europe reported of the many ships they saw anchored off the shore of Limassol waiting to take onboard cargos of wine for export to Venice and other European destinations. One of them, Sibthorp, described Limassol in 1787 as "an *insignificant city that some people visit only because it is next to the Commandaria wine growing area.*"[14]

Profit was not the only motive for shipping Commandaria to Europe. The Hospitallers established a sovereign state in

---

[14] Cobham, *Excerpta Cypria*, Cambridge, 1908, p. 329

Rhodes, but they continued to own properties and estates in Spain, France, England and elsewhere, many of which belonged previously to the Order of the Temple. In France, they owned hundreds of fiefs, priories, and estates of every kind. All these were managed by local commanders appointed by the Grand Master. The result was a complex system of interdependencies and cooperation, including in the sourcing of products such as wine and sugar that were needed everywhere but could only be produced in some places. The wine of Cyprus, being of special quality and having the ability to withstand transport and to improve with time, was in great demand within the Order too. A century earlier, the wine of Cyprus had found its way to the French court and had won a prize. Now it became a precious commodity that was very popular, even among the senior clergy of the Catholic Church.

Sourcing the wine in Cyprus was not always easy, because production and export were controlled by the king, who always gave priority to meeting the needs of his own court and the local aristocracy. Although production increased to levels previously unforeseen in the 14th century (see the data presented in the next chapter), demand continued to exceed supply and the kings of Cyprus sometimes had to impose restrictions on exports. And, when Venice gained control over Cyprus in the second half of the 15th century, the Knights of Rhodes had to exert all their influence to secure the quantities required to cover their needs in Rhodes and elsewhere.[15]

In view of the 'international' character of the Order of St. John, and the need to secure their own supplies from places and estates lying wide apart, the 'export' of wine from Cyprus and

---

[15] Nicholas Coureas, ob.cit., 2013

its movement across the seas may have not always been a commercial activity in the real sense. Whatever its character, it is this 'mobility' that made Commandaria known everywhere in Europe and ensured it was in great demand in many places and markets.

CHAPTER V

14TH CENTURY: THE GOLDEN AGE OF COMMANDARIA

The historical context of the period

The 14th century can justly be called the golden age of Commandaria. Several sources document the significant expansion of vine plantations and the rich income that wine production brought to the royal family and to the nobles of Cyprus. We have already referred to the owe felt by Rudolf von Südheim around 1340 AD when he visited the extensive vineyards of Phinikas near Paphos and of Colos near Limassol. Both belonged to the Hospital but were near the coast, far from the Grand Commandery's main vineyard in the hilly eastern part of today's Limassol District that extended over 31 villages and settlements, reaching up to the Troodos Mountain range.

Before moving on to present the extensive data contained in Vatican archive documents on the economic geography of southern Cyprus in the mid-14th century, it is perhaps important to describe, in short, the wider historical context of this period.

The golden age of Commandaria coincided with the highest point of the Cypriot kingdom's strength and prosperity which was reached during the reign of King Peter I (1359-1369 AD). From a young age, Peter was a staunch supporter of the crusades and, in 1347, his father, Hugh IV, put him in isolation in the castle of Kyrenia on the north coast to avoid any actions that would endanger the kingdom's safety and peace. It is there that Peter founded the Order of the Sword enlisting other young enthusiasts who swore to always remain faithful to him and to the cause of the Cross. They undertook to act "in secrecy, moderation and wisdom, without talking much and without promising much".[16] When Peter succeeded his father to the throne in 1359, the time was ripe for realizing his grand designs. Responding to a call for help by the Kingdom of Lesser Armenia on the Cilician coast, he occupied the stronghold of Corykos and repulsed the repeated attacks of the Mamluks. In 1361, he defeated the Emir of Tekke and captured the city of Antalya. Soon after, he turned the rest of the Turkish Emirs of southern Asia Minor into his vassals. In 1362, he left for Europe to rally support for a major crusade. He passed through Avignon, where he secured the support of the new Pope, Urban V, and on the 6th of November, he arrived in London. There, he was the guest of honour during the famous "Feast of the Five Kings" held in the English capital on the occasion of a major gathering of European sovereigns. Other than that, he didn't achieve much in London. Neither did he receive any genuine support from the German Emperor and the King of Poland when he visited them in Krakow the next year. However, having secured the support of the Pope and, through him, of some French forces and the Order of St. John with their fleet, Peter attacked and captured Alexandria in October 1365. He could keep it for only three days, but this made him appear as a powerful king and a defender of the faith. In 1368, he was offered the Crown of Armenia too and became the first king to claim possession of three royal

---

[16] Janet Shirley και Peter Edbury, *Guillaume de Machaut, The Capture of Alexandria*, Aldershot, 2001.

crowns: of Jerusalem, Cyprus, and Armenia. One year later, he lost his life in a dispute with his own barons on womanizing issues. The Order of the Sword soon lost its military character and was turned into a ceremonial society, theoretically pursuing the preservation of the Christian Kingdom of Cyprus under the Lusignan dynasty. Twenty-five years later, we have the first evidence of a European traveller becoming a member (and thus knighted) just by promising to come to the rescue of Cyprus if ever it was threatened by the Turks.

Losing a king as strong as Peter marked the beginning of a long period of decline of the Frankish kingdom of Cyprus. His widow, Eleanor of Aragon, asked for the help of the Genoese, presumably to revenge the death of her husband, and allowed them to occupy the important trading city of Famagusta; they kept it for 100 years.

They won thus an enormous advantage over their rivals, the Venetians, who had to content themselves with the estate and sugar mills of Episkopi, opposite Colos, in return for a substantial loan granted to King Peter by Frederick Cornaro in 1364 to finance his military campaigns. A daughter of this family, Catherine Cornaro, functioned as a Trojan horse for Venice when she married King James II of Cyprus in 1472. Succeeding him upon his suspicious death a year later, she finally gave up her throne in 1489 in favour of her "mother country".

The production of Commandaria in royal domains in the 14th century; the flourishing internal market

The evidence concerning wine production and consumption in the 14th century suggests that a denomination such as "royal wine" might have been more appropriate than Commandaria, given that the quantities produced in royal domains and in the fiefs allocated to other members of the royal family and to the barons making up the royal court in Nicosia were much bigger than those of the Commanderies of St. John. Nicosia was a major market in those days and absorbed considerable quantities, probably far beyond those taken out of the country by the Knights of Rhodes.

In fact, the kings of Cyprus depended to a considerable extent on the proceeds from the sale of wine, and it is for this reason that the traditionally most important wine-growing areas to the south of the Troodos Mountain range were turned into royal domains from the beginning of the Frankish period.

These are, in essence, the conclusions drawn from two important documents from this period that we will now examine. But before doing so and to have a basis for comparison, it is useful to review the information about the revenue of the Order of St. John in Cyprus. Two Vatican archive documents from the year 1419/20[17] give us perhaps the most reliable estimate of this. They put the yearly income of the Hospitallers in Cyprus at over 60 000 bezants. Assuming that roughly one-sixth of this amount was coming from the Small Commanderies of Finikas-Anogyra and Templos, described before, there remain 50 000 bezants which is a good approximation of the revenue of the Grand Commandery of Colos in a single year.

In 1962, the French academic Jean Richard published a series of previously unknown documents from the Vatican

---

[17] Jean Richard, *Chypre sous les Lusignans: Documents Chypriotes des Archives du Vatican (XIVe et XVe siecles,* Paris, 1962

Archives concerning medieval Cyprus. Among them was the famous "Compte de Bernard Anselme" (Accounts of Bernard Anselme from the year 1368). This Latin ecclesiastic of the Diocese of Limassol had recorded all receipts and expenses of the Latin Diocese of Limassol for the year 1367-1368.[18]

Limassol's Latin bishop, Guy d'Ibelin, had died on 29 March 1367 and, until a new bishop was appointed, the Diocese was obliged, according to the custom of the Catholic Church, to report to the Holy See its financial inflows and outflows. The primary source of income of a Catholic Diocese in those days was the tithe, a kind of church tax payable in cash or in kind, which amounted to 10% of all incomes earned in the Diocese. Nobody was exempt from this tax, neither the king, nor the nobles, nor the Latin monasteries, nor the properties of chivalric and other religious Orders, despite their occasional claims.

The information in Bernard Anselme's accounts is of truly inestimable value. By multiplying the amount of the tithe by 10, one receives a more or less accurate estimate of a taxpayer's total income. Taxpayers are mentioned by name and village and there is much more information coming out of the description of the Diocese's payments to cover its own costs.

As shown by the map published by Jean Richard, the Diocese of Limassol was quite large and extended from the ridge of Mount Afames in the West, to Asomatos and Mount Stavrovouni in the East.

---

[18] Jean Richard, *Chypre sous les Lusignans: Documents Chypriotes des Archives du Vatican (XIVe et XVe siècles)*, II. Le diocèse de Limassol d'après le compte de Bernard Anselmee (1367) – Le compte de Bernard Anselmee, Paris, 1962.

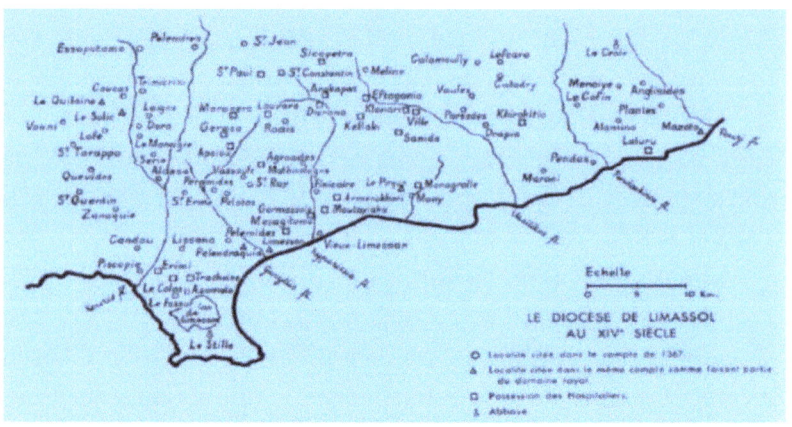

The Diocese of Limassol in the 14th century (from Jean Richard, 1962)

Concerning the revenues associated with wine production and sale, it suffices to present the information summarised by Jean Richard in his notes preceding the actual presentation of the detailed entries in the accounts.

"Of the 100 000 bezants that the king received annually in the Diocese of Limassol, the largest part came from the village estates: close to 86 500 in 1367. It is to the king that belonged the fief of Quilaine (Kilani) where one of the most famous vineyards of the island was located. It brought to the king no less than 29 000 bezants. The one of Solic (Silikou), next to it, brought almost the same."

Several other entries in the accounts of Bernard Anselme confirm the information in many other documents, namely that the primary source of revenue of the royal fiefs of Kilani and Silikou was the production and sale of wine.

It is impressive to have such clear evidence that these two villages, famous since ancient times for producing excellent wine, yielded together over 50% of the royal revenue in the vast Diocese of Limassol, perhaps even more than the Grand Commandery of Colos which comprised close to 40 villages, including seven in the most fertile lowlands west of Limassol.

The two royal estates were managed by so-called *apautors,* who signed contracts with the royal treasury, the *sécréte*, and undertook to pay the church tax directly to the Diocese of Limassol. We even know their names: Philip Cappadocha for Kilani and Jacob Quinnamos for Silikou.

In both villages, there were also "free vineyards" (*vignes franches*), a rare phenomenon for the Latin East. According to Jean Richard, these were estates belonging to persons other than the owners of the fiefs and were managed independently. In the Accounts of Bernard Anselme, we find separate entries for their tithe payments to the Diocese, most of them in kind. No names are mentioned for Silikou, but for Kilani there is reference to a Nikolas Romanos and a George Archdeacon. All these names sound very Greek and Jean Richard assumes that Quinnamos and Archdeacon were local burgers of Greek origin. Strange that he left out the other two, whose names were common Greek family names in those days and even today.

The above findings and names strongly suggest that Greek members of the Frankish *bourgeoisie*, probably descendants of the Byzantine Archons who owned these rich estates before 1192, had found a new role under the feudal system of land tenure.

The evidence further suggests that the very high revenues of the royal fiefs of Kilani and Silikou were deriving from Commandaria production. Kilani is identical with the Quilaine that De Mas Latrie put in place of Quillac when presenting for the first time in 1837 the wording of Article 5 of the constitution adopted by the Knights of St. John in the year 1300 in Limassol. In a footnote to the text, this famous French historiographer noted: "Quilaine, *a village north of Limassol, on the antipodes of Mount Olympus, which is still rich in vines today. The wine produced on the southern slopes of Mount Olympus, from Troodos to Machairas and Stavrovouni, is in particularly high demand under the name Commanderia inherited from our knights.*"[19]

Geographically, the Kilani wine growing area covers the biggest part of the valley stretching from north to south between Mount Afames to the West and the mountain ridge separating it from the neighbouring Kouris valley to the East. According to Jean Richard, the 14th century Kilani mentioned in the accounts of Bernard Anselme probably included the area of today's Vouni, established later, and that of some dependent settlements that have vanished in the meantime (Agios Andronikos and Asomatos of Kilani).

The medieval fief of Silikou, covered only the western bank of the Kouris River and not even all of it. The accounts also refer to Siria, a fief to the south of Silikou, known to have been granted by King Peter I to John Lascaris, one of his closest associates and a member of the Order of the Sword. Siria and the "free vineyards" of Silikou appear in the accounts as separate taxpayers, and so do the three villages taking up the eastern bank of the Kouris valley (Lania, Doros and Monagri), which belonged to other well-known barons of 14th-century Cyprus.

How could then Silikou yield such a high income to the royal family? There is only one explanation for this finding.

---

[19] De Mas Latrie, *Histoire de l'il le de Chypre*, 2, Paris, 1837, p. 90

Demand for good quality Commandaria must have been very high, putting pressure on privileged locations like Silikou and Kilani to increase production as much as possible. Silikou's vineyards must have been much more extensive than the area used for agricultural production today, covering even the steeper slopes of the surrounding mountains. Remnants of the stone walls built to support the medieval vine terraces can still be seen today.

The accounts of Bernard Anselme also contain evidence of extensive vine planting in places of even higher altitude such as Pelendri. Nowadays, a part of this village's area is covered with forest trees, but this was not the case in 1367. The fief of Pelendri belonged to the king's brother John, the nominal Prince of Antioch. According to Jean Richard, in 1367 the fief of Pelendri paid to the Diocese of Limassol a tithe of 856 measures of wine. A measure (from Greek metra) is equivalent to 25 litres approximately. This tithe corresponds therefore to an estimated total production of 214 000 litres or 2140 hectolitres of wine. Although this is only about half the quantity of Silikou, estimated by Constantinou (2016),[20] it still requires a vast vineyard to be produced. No wonder that the Diocese of Limassol felt the need to ask the Latin prior of Silikou, James Boudric, to go up to Pelendri in the autumn of 1367 and seal the earthen jars containing the tithe. Jean Richard estimated the annual earnings of the Prince of Antioch from the fief of Pelendri and of several dependent properties around it, to be in the Order of 15 000 bezants annually.

In the Accounts of Bernard Anselme, we also find an entry about the sale of 146 measures of wine from Pelendri which

---

[20] Antonis Constantinou, *ob.cit.*, Kedros, Athens, 2016

yielded 341 bezants in total or 2,33 bezants per measure. This is much higher than the price fetched from the sale of wine of diverse origins taken down to Limassol and sold in various markets. There, 187 measures yielded only 138 bezants (0,73 bezants per measure). The variation in price is a typical characteristic of a discerning market where good quality wine is sold at a premium.

Another piece of evidence from the Vatican Archives, also published by Jean Richard,[21][22] shows that Nicosia was a major market for wine in the 14th century and that good quality wine was fetching premium prices in the capital.

As we saw in the previous section, a considerable share of the annual tax payments to the Diocese of Limassol was made in kind. Very significant quantities of wine ended up in this way in the cellars of the Latin bishop in Limassol. One would have expected that when the movable and immovable property of Guy d'Ibelin was inventoried shortly after his death, a lot of this wine would have been found stored in his cellars. Jean Richard informs us, however, that this was not at all the case. Only four empty earthen jars (pithars) were found in his house in Limassol, whereas in Nicosia he owned several extensive cellars where he had stored very significant quantities of wine. One of them contained 39 large pithars with an average storage capacity of about 260 litres each. Three pithars were empty, but the rest contained 355 measures of "red wine from

---

[21] Jean Richard, *Un eveque d'Orient latin au XIVe siécle: Guy d'Ibelin, Eveque de Limassol, et l'inventaire de ses biens* (*Bulletin de corresp. hellenique*, t. LXXIV, 1950, p. 104).

[22] Jean Richard, "*Guy d'Ibelin, O. P., évéque de Limassol et l'inventaire de ses biens*", in *Les Relations entre l'Orient et l'Occident au Moyen Age*, Aldershot, Vol. 119, 1992, 1999.

the previous year" valued at 692 bezants. This is close to two bezants per measure, not far below the price fetched by the wine from Pelendri.

Two other cellars contained white wine, which was sold at an even higher price (2.24 and 2.33 bezants per measure, respectively). This premium price shows that it must have been aged Commandaria. As we saw in previous chapters, Commandaria assumed a yellowish colour with time and, as Stefano de Lusignan and Jovanni Mariti informed us, it acquired a pleasant smell and became really perfect.

Other than confirming the considerable variation in the price of Commandaria, depending on quality and vintage year, this data shows that Nicosia was a major market for premium quality wine in the 14th century. This is supported by another finding: while many of the fief owners in the Diocese of Limassol paid at least a part of their tithe in kind, the royal estates of Kilani and Silikou had no resort to this practice. They paid in cash, according to Bernard Anselme. Some authors wrongly understood this to mean that Kilani and Silikou were not producing wine. This is a rather superficial assessment of the data. How could the heart of Cyprus' wine growing area avoid producing Commandaria? And then, what was the source of their high revenues?

There is a very plausible explanation why they paid in cash whereas the "free vineyards" of both villages and all the surrounding estates paid in kind, at least partly. The wine of Kilani and Silikou was simply reserved for the royal family. With such high demand for premium wine in Nicosia, it wouldn't have been sensible for the king of Cyprus to let others lay hand on his own wine. The more so in the case of King Peter I, who went down in history as a "Christian Champion" spending much of his time visiting the monarchs of Europe to rally support for his crusading plans. In those times, it was usual for the kings and princes to exchange gifts on such occasions. What better idea could Peter conceive than to present his hosts with a few barrels of Commandaria, the "pope" of European wines? In fact, tradition wants Commandaria to have been flowing abundantly during the famous "Feast of the Five Kings" organized in London at the end of 1362 on the occasion of King Peter's presence in the English capital. It is worth reviewing in some detail the available historical evidence concerning this famous banquet.

Commandaria and the "Feast of the Five Kings": What really happened?

The "Feast of the Five Kings" is a seven-century old tradition of the City of London which was best described by the English historian C. L. Kingsford in 1916[23] after having discovered some relevant records in the House of Parliament. It is about a banquet from the year 1362/1363 arranged by Henry Picard, a former Lord Mayor of London, on the occasion of the presence in London of five European sovereigns. Besides Edward III of England, the other kings taking part in the Feast were Peter I of Cyprus, David II of Scotland, Jean II of France, and Valdemar IV of Denmark. Other sources add the Duke of Bavaria and a few other less important rulers.

Regrettably, the information reproduced in C.L. Kingsford's article is scarce and does not constitute a full account of the

---

[23] Charles Kingsford, *The Feast of the Five Kings*, in *Archaeologia 67* (1915-1916)

historical circumstances and the importance of the banquet. He describes in a poetic language the bets and games of the five kings and says little about the reasons for the presence of so many important rulers in the capital of England. Fortunately, there is sufficient evidence from other historical sources allowing us to have a good picture about what was really happening and what was the occasion.

We know, for example, that Henri Picard was not just a former major of London but a vintner, a merchant of wine, and the leader of an association of traders, who were interested to be officially appointed by the King of England as suppliers of wine to the court and to the City of London. It seems that their investment in the symposium paid off handsomely. In 1363, King Edward granted them a license to import wine from Gascogne in the Duchy of Aquitaine in today's France which belonged to the Crown of England until the middle of the 15th century. Henri Picard's "Worshipful Company of the Vintners in the City of London" survived to the present day and is one of London's 12 most ancient and respected "livery companies".

However, with time, it assumed a character that is more cultural and ceremonial than commercial. Still, the "Feast of the Five Kings" continues to be celebrated as the company's most important tradition and even their seat, "Vintners Hall", is housed in the stately City of London's "House of the Five Kings". The interior of the building is adorned with many works of art, including a stained window and a copy of Albert Chevallier Tayler's painting of 1920, both depicting the banquet of the five kings. Tayler's painting was, in fact, presented by the society to the Royal Exchange of London a hundred years ago and it stands there until today.

The Emblem of the Worshipful Company of the Vintners in the City of London

Stained window depicting the 'Feast of the Five Kings' in the seat of the 'Worshipful Company of the Vitners of London', in the City of London.

In this booklet, however, we deal with the history of Commandaria and not with the traditions of an English livery company. In fact, these traditions say nothing about the role that Commandaria had played during the Feast of the Five Kings, although it is almost certain that it did. The five kings did not gather in London to discuss the trade in wine, but the plans of the King of Cyprus for a new crusade. We know that Peter I set off in 1362 on a tour of European courts to rally support for his holy cause. After securing the support of Pope Urban V, he arrived in London on the 6th of November of the same year. In those days, it was difficult for five kings to come together and therefore the banquet we are talking about may have taken place towards the end of 1362 or the beginning of 1363. Whatever the timing, it was the visit of the King of Cyprus that provided the occasion for this gathering.

A similar gathering of European sovereigns took place in Krakow, Poland in 1363. The Emperor of Germany, the King of Poland and 12 other rulers from Central Europe arrived there to welcome the King of Cyprus and to hear about his plans. Peter I was not viewed, as one would think today, as the king of a small island kingdom, but as one of the most powerful sovereigns in Europe and a Champion of the Christian cause. No European ruler could afford to ignore his calling.

The London sources about the Feast of the Five Kings say nothing about Commandaria, but they don't say much about anything else either. There is another tradition, a persistent one, that speaks about Commandaria having been celebrated at the Feast as the *"king of the wines and the wine of the kings"*. In fact, one could hardly imagine Peter I arriving in Europe to rally the support of all major European rulers without carrying presents for them. What other present would have been more *"fit for royals*" than the famous Commandaria wine of his homeland that was declared the "pope of wines" a century earlier?

A digression into local history: The valley of the river Kouris during the golden age of Commandaria

Nothing is perhaps more indicative of the 14th century being the golden age of Commandaria than the findings confirming the central role of the Kouris valley in the production of wine. Wine was produced in this beautiful sun-drenched valley since time immemorial and it wouldn't be an overstatement to call it the cradle (or at least one of the cradles) of wine production in the world. An extensive area within the valley, over both sides of the river, bears to the present day the name of Dionysus, the ancient Greek God of wine. The biggest natural spring of Silikou is known as 'Lavrania' deriving from a local denomination of Zeus, 'Lavranios Dias'.

It was not by chance that the early Frankish kings of Cyprus turned the western bank of the Kouris valley into a royal domain and distributed the lands on the eastern one to some of their closest associates. Today's three villages flanking the river Kouris on the eastern side are also mentioned in the Accounts of Bernard Anselme from the year 1367 and this allows us to trace their background. Lania belonged to Jacob Scandelion whose daughter Echive was a mistress of king Peter I. Neighbouring Doros was owned by John de la Fierte, whereas nearby Monagri, apparently a bigger fief, was divided between four influential barons of the kingdom of Cyprus. They were Simon de Neville, Arnaude de la Plancharte, Stephanie Anthiome, and John de Giblet, all of them important figures of the time. John de Giblet was a scion of the prominent family of nobles originating in Byblos in today's Lebanon. The Giblet accompanied Guy de Lusignan to Cyprus in 1292 and their family played an important role in the affairs of the kingdom during the next three hundred years. In 1473, Tristan de Giblet was a leading figure of the coup d'état against the Venetian takeover. He continued his efforts to save the kingdom of Cyprus and he even managed to gain the support of Queen Catherine Cornaro before she was recalled back to Venice in 1489 marking the end of 300 years of Frankish rule under the Lusignan dynasty.

Monagri may have been a major fief in the Middle Ages but was still rather insignificant compared to Silikou which, as mentioned earlier, solemnly dominated the western bank of the extensive Kouris valley. The kings of Cyprus chose to settle there a significant number of Latin immigrant refugees forced to leave Syria at the end of the 12th century. The presence of Latin communities in the countryside of Cyprus was quite rare in those days. Reviewing the relevant literature, Jean Richard concluded that the influence of the Latin church was quite limited in rural Cyprus during the Frankish period. According to the Accounts of Bernard Anselme, there were only three Latin parishes in the whole area of the Diocese of Limassol: Silikou in the Kouris valley, St. George in Limassol and Alaminos near Larnaca. These parishes were served by a priest called prior, who nominally belonged to the clergy of the Diocese. This explains the use of the term priory for a Latin parish. The prior's duties were not only religious. He also acted as local representative of the Diocese, helping to collect the church tithe and to secure its financial interests.

In 1367, James Boudric, the prior of Silikou, undertook several "missions" in this respect. Other than to Pelendri, referred to earlier, he was sent to Monagri and to other places to collect and store the wine owed to the Diocese. Obviously, wine was acting as a replacement for money in those days. Demand was such that the Diocese felt assured it could turn the wine into cash when needed, at a profit, as we saw earlier.

Nothing, however, demonstrates more convincingly the financial attractiveness of wine production in those days than a comparison between Silikou and Alaminos. Both were Latin priories controlled by the royal family. In 1367, Silikou belonged to King Peter I and Alaminos to his brother John de Lusignan, Prince of Antioch. Silikou produced mainly wine and Alaminos mainly cereals. King Peter's revenue from Silikou was over 25 000 bezants while his brother had to content himself with 1400 bezants from Alaminos. The Prince of Antioch would have felt very poor if he did not own, besides Alaminos, the fief of Pelendri from where he was earning another 15 000 bezants a year by producing wine.

The history of medieval Silikou and of neighbouring Siria was reviewed by Antonis Constantinou in a scientific paper[24] and in his book mentioned earlier.[25]

Today, Siria (Syrka in the local dialect) is just an agricultural area and a locality within the bounds of the village of Silikou. Its rich past lives on in the popular tradition that it was once a "Frankish kingdom" and that here stood the "Houses of the Regina". It is very likely that the names Siria and Silikou (originally Silica) are just a paraphrase of the Latin names of Syria and Cilicia respectively, the likely places of origin of the Latin

---

[24] Antonis Constantinou, (*Cilicia and Syria in Cyprus: The Latin Priory of Silikou and the Casal of Syrka in historical sources)*, Yearbook of the Cyprus Scientific Society for Historical Studies, 14, *2021,* pp 443-54.

[25] Antonis Constantinou, *ob.cit.,* Athens, 2016.

refugees settled in the royal domain of Silikou shortly after the creation of the Frankish kingdom. The arrival in Cyprus of Latin refugees of Syrian origin is well documented. They integrated quickly into the indigenous national group of the Greeks.[26]

Originally, Siria (Syrka) may have been just a settlement of Syrian immigrants and not a separate fief. It cannot be excluded that it was only in 1365 AD that it became a stand-alone property, cut off from the royal domain of Silikou, when King Peter found himself in need to make a present to his close associate John Lascaris who arrived with him from the West. John Lascaris was a Byzantine adventurer expelled from his homeland, who became a close associate of Pope Urban V by allegedly trying to help him reunite the Eastern and Western Churches under his authority. King Peter met him in Venice in 1364 and accepted him in his royal Order of the Sword. Lascaris came to Cyprus in 1365 and took part in all the military campaigns of Peter I.

Siria never grew to the size of a big village. It was rather a vine growing area with many cellars gathered around some kind of wine-making facility. It passed at times to other close supporters of the kings of Cyprus, including Vera de Giblet, Lady in Waiting of Queen Catherine Cornaro (1473-1489). It seems that Vera convinced Catherine to go along with the plans of her brother Tristan de Giblet and Rizzo di Marino who acted as middlemen for King Ferdinand of Naples and his illegitimate son Alonso of Aragon, trying to arrange a marriage between her and Alonso in an effort to free Cyprus from the suffocating embrace of Venice. The affair forced Venice to recall Catherine back home in 1489 AD and to turn the island into a Venetian colony.

---

[26] George Hill, *History of Cyprus*, 2, Cambridge University, 1948.

Siria was abandoned after the Ottoman conquest and decayed for centuries until a small church was built there at the end of the 19th century. It was dedicated to the Virgin Mary and celebrated twice a year, offering an opportunity to the people living in the surrounding villages to come together. Otherwise, it was known to local farmers as a place with some ruins surrounded by fields and gardens sown with pieces of earthen jars. Oral reports speak of farmers who, until a few decades ago, were afraid to dig deeper or to plant vines for fear of finding objects of archeological value, in which case their land would be taken over by the Department of Antiquities.

Today, only a few remains are in place. They were described by Constantinou (2016) in his book. Of particular interest are the remains of an enormous wall, part of a building of unknown purpose. Summing up the evidence, Constantinou put forward the idea that the wall was part of a "linos", a full-fledged medieval wine making facility with a press.

This view is supported by other findings. Apparently, Siria availed of extensive subterranean cellars filled with pithars, earthen jars half-sunk into the ground as it is the custom to the present day. One of these jars (from now on referred to as the "pithar of Syrka") was unearthed by a Silikou farmer in 1956, fully intact and in usable condition. He refrained from informing the authorities and continued using it for storing wine along with other jars. He told his co-villagers that it contained a lot of "dry Commandaria" at the bottom, obviously a reference to the "mother of the wine" as the suspensions of the wine settling to the bottom were called in the past. It was this farmer's son who, sixty years later, noticed some strange signs on the surface of this pithar and sought the advice of experts. They soon found out that they were representations of the emblem of the royal Order of the Sword founded by King Peter I of Cyprus in 1347 AD (see picture below).

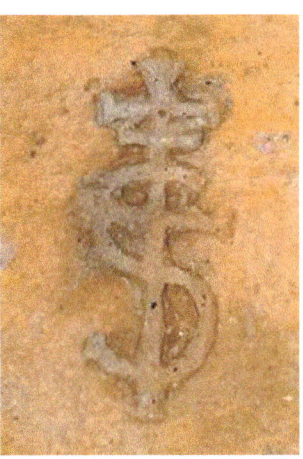

The "pithar of Syrka" and the emblem of the Order of the Sword engraved on its surface (courtesy of the 'Commandaria Museum', Silikou).

Besides the insignia of the Order of the Sword, there were three circles or wreaths on the pithar's surface that initially passed for simple decorations. It was Constantinou again who undertook to study the historical background of the Order of the Sword and to decipher the secrets of the "pithar of Syrka". He published his initial findings in the book cited before. In a more recent paper,[27] he attempted to put a timeframe in the construction and use of the pithar and to examine the likely purpose that the imprints on its surface had served.

---

[27] Antonis Constantinou, (*The emblem of the Order of the Sword and its representation on the pithar of Syrka: an attempt to date the pithar),* Yearbook of the Cyprus Scientific Society for Historical Studies, 15*, 2022, 13 pp.*

The three wreaths or crowns engraved on the surface of the "pithar of Syrka".

In view of the presence of the emblem of the Order of the Sword on the pithar's surface, the author concluded it would be naïve to consider the wreaths as simple decorations just because other jars carry small rings of the same shape too.

In French the word crown, *curonne*, also means wreath. The three wreaths could therefore well be crown representations and an allusion to the three crowns of the Lusignan dynasty: Cyprus, Jerusalem, and Lesser (Cilician) Armenia. Cyprus became officially a kingdom in 1197 AD when the Emperor of Germany sent a crown and a sceptre to Amalric, the brother and successor of Guy de Lusignan. This was their first crown. Long after Jerusalem was lost to the Christians in 1187, the nominal title "King of Jerusalem" continued to be contested by various Frankish nobles and, in 1268, King Hugh III of Cyprus won it, claiming a hereditary right. This was their second one.

Then, in 1368, the ailing kingdom of Cilician Armenia, desperately in need of support to avert its conquest by the Mamluks (which happened in 1375 AD anyway), offered its crown to the powerful king of Cyprus, Peter I. Peter accepted the offer and thus became the first Lusignan prince to hold three crowns at the same time. He proudly announced the acquisition of a third crown while touring in Europe in the same year. But he was assassinated early next year before being crowned. The Armenians chose Leo, another Lusignan prince, as their king and when he died in 1393 the crown returned to the Lusignan dynasty.

The question about the purpose of having a representation of the three Lusignan crowns on a wine jar unearthed in the Cypriot countryside proved to be a more difficult one. Clearly, an answer had to be sought in connection with the presence of the emblem of the Order of the Sword on the same jar.

Concerning the emblem, it is important to note first that such a representation was never found in Cyprus before. In his book *The Knights of the Crown: The Monarchical Orders of Knighthood in Later Medieval Europe*, D'Arcy Jonathan Boulton lists the various places where a depiction of the emblem of the Order of Cyprus was seen. All of them are located abroad.[28] Another author, Christiane Van Den Bergen-Pantens,[29] also described several places where a depiction of the Order's insignia was found, proving that several European nobles, including three majors of the city of Brussels,[30] had become

---

[28] D. D'Arcy Jonathan Boulton, *The Knights of the Crown: The Monarchical Orders of Knighthood in Later Medieval Europe, 1325-1520*, Great Britain, The Boydell Press, 2000.

[29] Van Den Bergen-Pantens, *Etude historique et iconographique de l'Ordre de l'Epee de Chypre*, in Melanges offerts a Zabolcs de Valvay, Braga livraria Cruz,1971, pp. 605-610.

[30] For the record, these were Antoine Thonis, Brussels major in 1391, 1402 and 1407; Henri t' Seraets, several times major between 1428 and 1467; and Nicolas Van den Heetvelde, also several times major around 1450 AD.

members in the 15th century. Again, none of the depictions were from Cyprus.

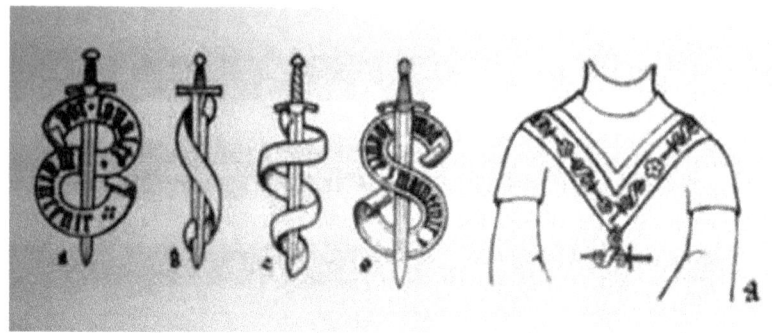

*Sketches of the insignia of the Order of the Sword
(from the book of D'Arcy Jonathan Boulton)*

Van den Bergen-Pantens presented evidence that a foreign visitor, Simon de Sarrebruck, was accepted into the Order as early as 1395.

Being knighted and carrying a necklace and jewels may have been socially prestigious in medieval Europe, but it had nothing to do with taking part in bloody campaigns, such as the one of 1365 against Alexandria. Both Christiane Van Den Bergen-Pantens and Jonathan Boulton therefore concluded that the Order of the Sword must have changed character sometime between the death of Peter I in 1369 AD and the year 1395 when Simon de Sarrebruck became a ceremonial member. Just like other monarchical Orders of the time, the reformed Order of the Sword assumed a symbolic character embodying the perseverance of the kingdom of Cyprus under the Lusignan dynasty. Candidates became members just by promising to come to the rescue of Cyprus, should it ever be threatened by the Muslims. By the time of Catherine Cornaro, almost every visitor to Cyprus had the opportunity to become a member of the Societatem Regum Cipri as the Order was then called. Felix Faber, a European traveller quoted by Boulton, gave us a full account. The Queen herself initiated the visitors into the Society and gave them small swords (gladiolos).

A comparison of Boulton's sketches of the insignia (emblem and necklace) with the engravings on the surface of the "pithar of Syrka" reveals important differences. The sketches in Boulton's book refer clearly to the period when the Order had only symbolic and ceremonial character. In contrast, Syrka's emblem seems to be more consistent with the information we have about the early years of the Order's life. The letter S is so perfectly formed and so symmetrical that one could hardly take it for a mere illustration of the ribbon that carried the slogan "pour loiauté maintenir". On the contrary, it supports the view of Felix Faber that it was denoting silence. And it is in line with the information in the poem of Guillaume de Machaut "*La prise d'Alexandrie*",[31] written in 1369, that the founder of the Order, King Peter I, demanded from its members "*to act secretly, with moderation and wisdom, without talking much and without promising too much.*"

Van Den Bergen-Pantens, who only knew the depictions of the Order's insignia from the period after 1395, did not agree that S denoted secrecy and dismissed the words of Guillaume de Machaut as poetic constructions. Strange, considering that when Peter I founded the Order in 1347 AD, he was living in isolation in the castle of Kyrenia because his father was afraid he might

---

[31] Janet Shirley και Peter Edbury, *Guillaume de Machaut, The Capture of Alexandria*, Aldershot, 2001.

exactly do what he did: start preparing for a crusade. Secrecy was, therefore, imperative. And in 1365, it was this adherence to the prerogative of secrecy and silence that enabled King Peter to surprise the garrison of Alexandria and capture the city.

Syrka's emblem pinpoints the initial period of the Order's life in more than one way. A royal crown stands at the top of the sword, underlining the central role of its founder and the loyalty its members owed to him. It alludes at the same time to some sort of connection to the papacy. The sword is crossed by two horizontal bars, one bigger than the other, forming the symbol of papal authority, the three-armed Cross. There is no mention of such a symbol in the literature concerning the ceremonial Order of the Sword. This again supports the view that the Syrka depiction was created during the reign of King Peter I. Peter had visited Pope Urban V in Avignon in 1362 and won his support for his planned crusade. The extra elements may have been added to the emblem to showcase the Pope's support and spiritual blessing.

The preceding analysis leads to the conclusion that the pithar of Syrka was likely constructed during the reign of Peter I, but not before 1368 when he had acquired the crown of Armenia. We know that after Peter's I death in 1369, the kingdom of Cyprus went through a period of chaos. His successor, Peter II, was just a child and his estranged wife, Eleanor of Aragon, invited the Genoese to interfere in the affairs of the kingdom, allegedly to revenge the assassination of her husband by his own barons. The change in the Order's of the Sword character and purpose must therefore have happened immediately after the death of its founder and was probably completed before 1395, when Simon de Sarrebruck was accepted as a 'ceremonial' member.

Returning now to Siria or Syrka, we note that the construction of new earthen jars (pithars) would make sense if we assume that it was turned into a separate fief in 1365 specifically to be given to John Lascaris. The property may have been small but the presence of so many cellars in the surrounding fields shows clearly that it was still producing considerable quantities of wine. This is another indication that the 14th century was a golden age for Commandaria.

It remains to explain the purpose of imprinting the insignia of a royal Order on the surface of the "pithar of Syrka". Constantinou (2023) analysed thoroughly the historical evidence referring to the particular place and time and came up with a simple, down-to-earth explanation: <u>The purpose of the imprints was to avert confiscation of Siria's wine harvest in a legal dispute. In those days, wine was so precious that it functioned as a liquid financial asset.</u>

The owner may have been someone who simply wanted to showcase his membership of the prestigious Order of the Sword and the full support he enjoyed from both the powerful King Peter I (the holder of three crowns) and the even more powerful Pope Urban V of Avignon (the holder of the three-armed Cross).

He must have been under a lot of pressure to do so. But this is exactly the situation in which John Lascaris, the owner of the fief, found himself in 1367/68.

There is a rich bibliography about the life and estate of this Byzantine adventurer, including in the chronicle of Leontios Machairas. It was reviewed and presented by D. Jacoby in an extensive article in the Review of Byzantine Studies, vol. 26 of 1968.[32]

Lascaris was branded as a dowry seeker and was declared *persona non grata* in Constantinople after having had an affair

---

[32] David Jacoby, «Jean Lascaris Calophéros, Chypre et la Morée», *Revue des Études byzantines*, 26, 1968, σσ. 189-228.

with a niece of Emperor Palaeologus. He ended up in the West, where he convinced the Pope that he could help him reunite the Churches under his leadership. He became a member of the Order of the Sword and arrived in Cyprus in 1365 to take part in King Peter's I crusading campaigns.

He was in fact on Peter's galleon during the attack and capture of Alexandria in October 1365 and, in 1367, he commanded one of the 29 galleys that sailed to Antalya in present-day Turkey, which was a Cypriot possession from 1361 to 1373, in order to suppress a rebellion against its commander. He also took part in other military and pirate adventures of Peter I between 1365 and 1368.

In March 1366, Lascaris married Maria Maimars, widow of Jean de Soissons. She undertook to pay to him as a dowry the astronomical sum of 243 567 bezants. Unable to find the money, she transferred to him the entire estate of her late husband. She did so with the consent of Peter I, as mentioned in a letter of Pope Gregory XI from the year 1376 supporting Lascaris' claims. However, this act was not in agreement with the feudal law of the time and was not accepted by Soissons' children. After the assassination of Peter I on 17 January 1369, and Maria Maimars' death a few months later, Janot de Soissons confiscated his father's assets with the support of his sisters Alise, wife of Baudouin de Nores, and Marquerit, wife of Léon de Lusignan. All three families belonged to the upper aristocracy of Cyprus. Despite repeated interventions by Pope Urban V and his successor Gregory XI in his favour, Lascaris ended up at some stage in prison and in 1372 was forced to leave Cyprus.

According to Jacoby, the fief of Siria had been granted to Lascaris directly by his friend and protector Peter I and should not logically have been the subject of his dispute with the

Soissons. However, their financial differences were very serious, and it is not excluded that the Soissons eyed Siria's wine as a liquid asset that they could confiscate, just as the Diocese of Limassol confiscated wine when the tithe owed to it was not paid in time.

In Cyprus, Lascaris presented himself as a kind of representative of the papal authority, the full support of which he enjoyed. It is therefore possible that, further to his differences with the Soissons, he had refused (or was unable) to pay his ecclesiastical tax to the Diocese of Limassol, just as the Knights of St. John had done on various occasions, claiming that they were part of the Church.

In Bernard Anselme's 1367 register, Lascaris is listed as taxable (for his Siria income) but no amount of money is mentioned. If Lascaris had in fact refused to pay his tithe, it is likely that the local representative of the Diocese of Limassol, the prior of Silikou James Boudric, confiscated the wine that owed to the Church (or threatened to confiscate it). Such confiscations were not unusual in those times. Even John de Lusignan, the brother of King Peter I, was not except from such reprisals. In the Accounts of Bernard Anselme there is mention of a visit by Boudric to Pelendri, John's fief, to seal the pithars containing the wine of the tithe. Boudric did the same in Monagri in 1367. In another case, he went to Cormya, near today's Vouni, to confiscate valuables against unpaid taxes.

John Lascaris had indeed powerful reasons to mark Sirias' pithars as belonging to someone who was a friend of both the King and the Pope and a member of the glorious Order of the Sword. When his protector died, nothing could save him. He ended up in prison and had to leave Cyprus. Even worse. His reputation was stained for good. Soon after he left Cyprus, he married by letter Lucie, the daughter of Erard III Mavros, Lord of Arcadia in the Frankish Morea. Before the marriage was "consumed", he found himself in a legal dispute with his father-in-law about Lucie's dowry and the contract they had signed. Erard III even confiscated the goods that Lascaris had brought from Cyprus and it was only with the help of the Pope again that he managed, three years later, to have access to his wife and to produce a son.

CHAPTER VI

FORTIFIED COMMANDARIA AND THE *VINUM MAROALI*: VENTURING INTO THE LATIN VOCABULARY

The senior Latin clergy of Cyprus as 'ambassadors' of Commandaria

The royal house of Cyprus and the Knights of St. John were not the only 'ambassadors' of the sweet wine of Cyprus abroad. The Latin clergy also helped to spread Commandaria's fame to many other countries.

Nicholas Coureas, the Cypriot historian of the Middle Ages, cited in a recent article several Latin Church documents from the 14th century that mentioned a type of Cypriot wine of hitherto unknown origin called "Maroa".[33] The name "Maroa" appeared first in a document connected with the incarceration between December 1329 and January 1330 in the Dominican House of Nicosia of a certain Arnald de Fabriciis, a Franciscan brother and Papal Legate. Perhaps because of his status, Fabriciis was treated well while in prison. The records of the inquisition mention that he was allowed "to eat

---

[33] Nicholas Coureas, *Food, wine and the Latin clergy of Lusignan Cyprus (1191-1473)*, in *Multidisciplinary approaches to food and foodways in the medieval Eastern Mediterranean*, 2020, edited by Sylvie Yona Walksman, ARCHÉOLOGIE (S)// 4

meat, eggs, chicken, cockerels, and fish and to drink good 'Maroa' wine".

A few years later, the name "Maroa" appeared in the observations of the Augustinian friar James of Verona, who visited Cyprus in 1335. He stated that a wine called "Marea" (obviously identical with "Maroa") was so strong that it could only be consumed when mixed with four parts of water.

Some decades later, "Maroa" even attracted the attention of the papal curia in Avignon. In April 1372, a priest of Nicosia received 200 bezants in *bonis grossis et legalibus* (in good and legal *gros* coins) to purchase some *vinum maroali* for the papal curia.

Summarizing the evidence concerning "Maroa", Nicholas Coureas concluded that the wine of Cyprus *"enjoyed such a good reputation among the 14th century Latin clergy of Cyprus, that its fame spread well beyond the confines of the island."*

In search of the origin and characteristics of "Maroa" wine

Other than the timing (14th century), its name and the information that "Maroa" was very strong, we have no other information about this type of wine. So far, the name did not appear in any other source. However, the description of James of Verona of this wine being "so strong it could not be consumed unless mixed with four parts of water" is not the only one we come across in the literature.

We have already mentioned the way Stephen de Lusignan described the quality of the wines of Cyprus in his first book that appeared in Bologna in 1573.[34] From this description, we note the passage concerning very old wines. *"Some of our nobles"*, he says, *"have wines 60 to 80 years old. Very old wine burns like oil and can even be used as a balm. But to drink it you need five fingers of water for each finger of wine and even then, you have difficulty swallowing it, so strong it is."*

Cornelis van Bruin, a Dutch traveller to Cyprus, writing in 1683[35] describes the old wines of Cyprus in the following words: *"I have drunk wine here that is over 30 years old: it had a pleasant taste and an exquisite colour and was so dense that it stuck to the glass just like 'eau de vie'. You can find wine up to 100 years old, because, when a father marries his child, he presents it with a vessel of the best wine he has, and when the wine runs low, they refill the vessel with wine of the same kind, and thus it preserves its original quality, and the older the better. But it is so strong that for normal use you must add twice as much water as wine. I don't remember having ever tasted a stronger wine."*

One hundred years later, Jovanni Mariti, who stayed in Cyprus for several years and studied exhaustively the island's wines and winemaking practices, qualifies the statements of Van Bruin. *"The oldest wines on the market"*, he says, *"are eight to ten years old. It is not true, as some in Europe believe, that one can find wine 100 years old."*[36]

And he gives the details we have described in Chapter I about the custom of putting aside a jar full of wine at the birth of

---

[34] Lusignano di Cipro, Stefano Fr., *Chorograffia: et breve historia universale dell'Isola de Cipro principiando al tempo di Noè per in sino al 1572*, Bologna, 1573. (Translated to English by Olimpia Pelosi (State University of New York, 2001).

[35] In Claude Delaval Cobham, *Excerpta Cypria*, Cambridge, 1908, p. 241-242.

[36] Giovanni Mariti, *Viaggi per l' isola di Chipro*, Lucca, 1769 (partly translated and presented in Claude Delaval Cobham, *Excerpta Cypria*, Cambridge, 1908, p. 243-245)

a child to be consumed at his wedding party when grown up. It is thanks to Mariti that we know many other details about winemaking and production in Cyprus in the 18th century. He tells us, for example, that all liqueur wine produced in Cyprus was called Commandaria, although only about one fourth of it originated in the former area of the Commandery of St. John. And that Cyprus also produced table wines, of which the best was that of the village of Omodhos.

Despite all his knowledge, Mariti says nothing about the alleged strength of old Commandaria and the need to mix it with water. Either he didn't agree with the statements or, more likely, he didn't have access to such wine. As he himself says, *the oldest wines on the market are eight to ten years old.*

Notwithstanding Mariti's views, the information presented above points to a strong association between the age of Commandaria and its strength. In all cases where the wine was described as very strong and in need of being mixed with water, the wine was very old. Young Commandaria typically contains about 15% alcohol. It is hardly possible to produce wine with more than 15% alcohol by natural methods. Aging alone cannot change the alcohol content of wine and make it 'non-drinkable unless mixed with water'.

All this leads us to suspect that Commandaria destined for aging was fortified with the addition of grape alcohol to help the wine keep for a much longer time. Adding grape alcohol to the wine not only makes it much stronger, but it also helps the wine keep much longer without losing its basic characteristics. If applied at the right stage in the vinification process, it also helps to maintain a wine's sweetness, which, in those times, was desirable. This may help to explain the information quoted before that the nobles of the Frankish period often availed of wine 60 to 80 years old. Apparently, a 'normal' wine would be useless as a *"balm"* and for *"treating sick people"*; it wouldn't *"burn like oil"*; neither would it *"stuck on the glass like eau de vie"*.

Alcohol must have been readily available to fortify the wine. Zivania, a type of *eau de vie de vin* with typically 45-50% alcohol, but going up to 75%, has always been produced in the villages of Cyprus in considerable quantities as a by-product of winemaking and continues to be so to the present day. The peasants use it for various purposes: as a drink, as a disinfectant, as an aid for a good massage to relieve pain, and to facilitate a quick recovery in case of cold. It is likely that they also used it to ensure that the wine they 'hid' away for the wedding of their children would keep for as long as it would be necessary. Cypriot peasants were veritable experts in hiding away their produce to avoid confiscation for taxation or other purposes. Jovanni Mariti observed in the 18th century that the villagers buried their jars in the ground so skillfully that *"no one could imagine that below his feet there was an entire cellar with Commandaria"*.

For the other citizens, no matter their rank, such an old fortified and fully mature wine that had preserved its sweetness must have been a rare good that only a privileged few could lay their hands on. In the 18th century, Jovanni Mariti couldn't. No wonder, however, that in the height of the Frankish rule, the 14th century, the Latin clergy and even the Pope wanted to have a share of it.

It is highly probable that "Maroa" was a designation for such a rare wine. But we must still explain the meaning of the word, which, as mentioned before, is not found anywhere else in the literature.

All three documents where the name "Maroa" occurs were prepared by Catholic ecclesiastics, who spoke and used Latin as a routine. Maroa or Marea does not occur in Latin. However, according to the 1982 Oxford Dictionary of Latin, Maro, once a name of the Roman poet Virgil, was used figuratively through the ages in Italy and Rome to denote an outstanding poet. Was *vinum maroali* an expression used by the Latin clergy to denote figuratively an outstanding wine that, like a poet, was "*speaking to the heart*"? This is how Stephen de Lusignan described the wine of his homeland when he said that "*the wine of Cyprus is sweet, refined, tasty, strong and speaks to the heart.*" It was this same wine that in 1223, during the Paris wine contest, was figuratively called the "*pope of wines*". Why should we be surprised if it was also called the "*Maro of wines*", in Latin "vinum maroali"?

CHAPTER VII

TRADE IN COMMANDARIA THROUGH THE CENTURIES

Trade relations of the kingdom of Cyprus and the role of the Hospitaller estates

Cyprus lies at the crossroads of trade between East and West and played an important role in commercial exchanges since ancient times. Trade with the West was well-developed before the arrival of the Franks to Cyprus. Following the conclusion of a treaty with the Byzantine emperor John Comnenus in 1126, Venetian traders settled in Cyprus, notably in Limassol, which was the island's biggest commercial port until the end of the 13th century. Although most of their properties and houses in and around Limassol were confiscated by the Crown when the Latin kingdom of Cyprus was established in 1192, they were soon granted new concessions along with other trading nations, cities and mercantile houses. A lively trade soon developed between Cyprus and the West that further expanded in subsequent centuries.

Nicolas Coureas quoted several notarial documents of the time containing agreements for the export of merchandise and agrarian goods from Cyprus to a variety of destinations, including Constantinople. Cyprus was also used for the transit of goods sourced in neighbouring countries and regions.

Most of the trade in agricultural products was in the hands of the Order of the Hospital. Already in 1210, the Hospitallers had received concessions from King Hugh I on the export of agrarian goods from the estates he had granted to them. After the fall of Acre in 1292, they transferred their seat to Cyprus and became increasingly involved in agriculture. And, when the Templars' were dissolved in 1212, the Hospitallers appropriated their Cypriot estates, earning great wealth by producing significant quantities of agricultural commodities, much of which was exported. By 1372, they owned over 60 *casali* (villages). From an inventory sent to them by King Janus in 1411, temporarily relieving them from paying the royal tithe, we learn that they produced sizable quantities of wheat, barley, pulses, beans, peas, flax, oats, carobs, millet, cotton, carrots, sesame, olives, indigo, almonds, and onions,[37] besides the processed products of sugar, molasses and wine. After transferring their seat to Rhodes in 1309, a significant proportion of this production left Cyprus to cover the food supplies of the Order and to be sold in foreign markets. In 1329, the Venetian Marino Sanudo estimated that one ninth of the Hospitallers' total income of 180,000 Florins derived from their Cypriot estates.

Demand for sugar and cotton, in particular, increased in Western Europe during the late fourteenth and early fifteenth century and this gave an extra boost to the Order's mercantile activities.

Other foreign traders settled in Cyprus also benefitted from this trade, as shown by the plethora of commercial transaction documents and notarial notes that survived to the present day.

---

[37] Luttrell, '*The Hospitallers in Cyprus after 1386*', pp. 5–6, 10–11, 15. (cited by Nicholas Coureas, *ob.cit.*, 2013)

The quasi-monopoly of the Hospital in the export of Commandaria before the Venetian takeover

As expected, notarial documents do not tell us much about trade in wine. This is because, in the 14th and 15th centuries, the Hospitallers enjoyed a quasi-monopoly in the export of wine, given that most of the quantities available for export originated in their own estates. Wine produced in royal domains was mostly consumed in Cyprus and enjoyed remunerative prices, especially in Nicosia, where most of the island's aristocracy was living. Not much of 'non-Hospital' wine was available for export.

The Hospitallers shipped most of the produce of their Cypriot Commanderies to their seat in Rhodes and from there to other destinations in France, Spain, England and other countries where they owned extensive properties organized in Commanderies. When there was a surplus they sold it to buyers outside the Order. Rhodes traded much more extensively with the Genoese, Catalans, Provençals and Florentines than with the dominant trading power of the time, Venice. In fact, on various occasions, the Hospitallers sided with Genoa, Venice's arch-rival and this angered the Venetians, who had always been eyeing the lucrative profits of the sugar, molasses and wine trade of Cyprus. Things started to change in 1365 when Frederik Cornaro was granted the estate and sugar mills of Episkopi, opposite Colos, in exchange for a large loan granted to Peter I. However, a few years later, the Genoese exploited the ambition of King Peter's widow, Eleanore of Aragon, who ostensibly sought to revenge the murder of her husband by his own barons in 1369 and asked for their help. They established themselves in Famagusta and controlled the city for almost a century, turning it into a Genoese trading centre and port.

Venice becomes the prime destination of Commandaria exports

Things changed radically when Catherine Cornaro of Venice married King James II of Cyprus in 1472 and, after his death in 1473, became a reigning queen. She was a queen only in name, always acting according to the "advice" of the representatives of Venice, who henceforth were quasi in charge of the finances and administration of the kingdom.

To gain control over trade flows and share in the important profits that the export of agricultural commodities entailed, the Venetians had to control first the Commanderies of the Hospital on Cyprus and this is exactly what they did.

Under pressure from Venice and at the request of Queen Catherine, her uncle Marco Crispo, the Hospitaller commander of Verona, was appointed to the Grand Commandery of Colos in November 1475. In 1485, he was succeeded by the Venetian Hospitaller Marco Malipiero, who was first appointed administrator and then commander of the Grand Commandery. From the beginning of the 16th century, a full line of Venetian Hospitallers and Cardinals connected to the Cornaro family controlled the three Commanderies of the Hospital on Cyprus. The Order's Grand Masters in Rhodes supported the appointment of Venetians to these posts, mindful not to allow their relations with Venice to deteriorate further, something that threatened to fully alienate the Hospital from its own estates on Cyprus.

The practical implications of these changes were quite serious. First, the annual 'responsion' paid by the commanders to the Order's treasury in Rhodes was drastically reduced and gradually assumed a nominal character. Second, the taxes imposed on the agricultural produce of the Hospital's estates by the Queen (previously disputed or resisted by reference to the Hospital's religious status), now had to be paid in full, at least from 1525 onwards. And third, most of the Commanderies' exports were now destined for Venice. Shipments to other places, even to Rhodes, were made subject to ensuring that the needs of Venice were met as a matter of priority.

The control exercised by Venice over exports of agricultural produce from Hospitaller estates in Cyprus is exemplified by the way the Council of Ten responded to the requests of the Order's leadership[38] concerning their supplies from Cyprus. As early as March 1478, Grand Master Pierre d'Aubusson had to ask the Venetian government for permission to receive shipments of grain from his Order's estates in Cyprus. Another Grand Master, Emery d'Amboise, requested permission in 1506 to receive 10 000 *modia* of wheat and 10 000 *modia* of barley to meet his Order's needs on Rhodes. In its reply, the Council of Ten instructed the Venetian rectors in Cyprus to allow the export of 5000 *modia* of wheat and 10 000 *modia* of barley, but to do so only after ensuring that the quantities of grain stipulated by the Council were being sent to Venice, and without prejudice to the security of Cyprus.

On the other hand, as regards wine exports, this takeover by Venice was beneficial in several respects. Henceforth, wine was a real commercial commodity exported from Cyprus using established commercial channels and trade routes and not just a means of satisfying the needs of the Hospitaller knights in Rhodes and elsewhere.

---

[38] Nicholas Coureas, *A process of secularization? Venetian Hospitallers and Hospitaller estates in Cyprus after 1474*. In Ordines Militares Colloquia Torunensia Historica (Yearbook for the Study of Military Orders), 2016, pp. 111-126

Several visitors to Cyprus reported having seen many ships in the port of Limassol waiting to take onboard cargos of wine destined for Venice and elsewhere. From John Lock[39] and Tomasso Porcacchi[40], who were in Cyprus in 1553 and 1576 respectively, we learn that the biggest share of the production of Commandaria was shipped to Venice and was forwarded from there to other Italian provinces and to Rome.

Commandaria's exports continue during the Ottoman centuries: quantities, destinations and prices

Apparently, the established channels of trade with Venice continued to function after the Ottoman conquest of Cyprus in 1570/71. Exports to Venice and via Venice to Ragusa, Tuscany and other European destinations continued during the entire Ottoman period (1571-1878). In the meantime, Commandaria had become an important source of income for the island and its masters.

The wine was shipped in leather containers (*askia*), typically carrying about 750 litres, which were tarred inside to avoid leakage. The wine withstood the transport well, but acquired a light taste of tar which damaged its reputation. Cornelis van Bruin (1673), the Dutch traveller we have quoted before, was in fact very surprised to find out that in Cyprus itself this taste was not present. And he described the quality of Commandaria in the eloquent way we quoted earlier.

One of the most authoritative sources concerning the wines of Cyprus, Jovanni Mariti, the Italian abbot we have already

---

[39] Claude Delaval Cobham, *Excerpta Cypria*, Cambridge, 1908, p. 72
[40] Claude Delaval Cobham, *Excerpta Cypria*, Cambridge, 1908, p. 166

quoted several times, left us a very informative description of the pricing and destinations of Commandaria exports in the 18th century. "*Most of the wine is exported to Venice, where it is consumed even in coffee shops. However, the Venetians care little about quality, they never buy wine aged over 18 months, paying only one piastre per kouza (about 10,5 kg). The oldest and best quality wine is sent to Tuscany, France, and Holland where it fetches from two to three piastres per kouza. Of late, a considerable quantity of more common wine goes to Leghorn. It is exported in leather containers of 70 kouza. The export duties, together with the value of the container, amount to ten piastres.*"

Concerning the quantities exported in the 18th century, we have somehow conflicting evidence. Alexander Drummond, a Consul of His Majesty the King of England in Aleppo, Syria, who visited Cyprus in 1745, estimated total wine production at 800 000 *kouza* or 2,13 million gallons. Of these, 365,000 *kouza*, close to a million gallons were exported, mainly to Venice.[41]

Jovanni Mariti quotes quantities far below the above. "*Cyprus produces every year 40,000 kouza*", he says, "*and all the production takes its name from the "commanderia", which barely produces 10,000 kouza, but of the best quality. The rest comes from various areas of the island*".

Mariti informs us that Cyprus was producing other types of wine too, "*that are consumed with food, as in the Provence. The best ones come from the village of Omodhos.*" They were not exported but consumed on the island and on the ships that trade with Syria.

Mariti mentions specifically a muscat-type of wine but, again, his estimate of the quantity produced is modest. It hardly

---

[41] Claude Delaval Cobham, *Exerpta Cypria*, Cambridge, 1908, p. 281.

reaches 5000 *kouza*, he says, and it is sold at prices equal to those of Commandaria.

Considering that the first two centuries of Ottoman rule were characterized by economic decline and that Cyprus suffered a series of calamities because of disease, drought, and locust attacks, it is likely that the production of Commandaria had plummeted by the time Mariti was writing. However, the very considerable divergence between his figures and those of Drummond somehow make both less reliable. Closer to the truth appear to be the figures quoted by Michael de Vézin, another English Consul to Aleppo and Cyprus, whose notes were published in 1804. Vézin puts the production of Commandaria in the second half of the 18th century at 150 000 *kouza* and that of ordinary red wine at 175 000 *kouza*.[42]

Another British diplomat, William Turner, who visited Cyprus in 1815, speaks again of much lower quantities. 65 000 *kou*za, he says, were exported to Venice and the Black Sea, and another 40 000 *kouza* of inferior quality were consumed locally or channeled to Turkey.

Turner was aware of the unprecedented difficulties that Cypriot peasants and the countryside were facing in the early 19th century and that the population of the island had gone down considerably. In his own words, the people were living "in absolute misery". The situation deteriorated further because of the atrocities committed by the merciless Turkish governor Küçük Mehmet against the Christian population of Cyprus when the Greek revolution broke out in 1821. Impoverishment was widespread and Crypto-Christianism emerged again, at least temporarily, as a way of reducing the burden of taxation.

---

[42] Claude Delaval Cobham, *Exerpta Cypria*, Cambridge, 1908, p. 372.

The official Ottoman Census of 1831 confirmed the decimation of the rural population. To give an example, Silikou, once a flourishing royal estate and one of Cyprus' 20 biggest villages[43], now counted only 79 male taxpayers of which only one third were Christians.

Taxation and the way the cargos were organized

Beyond the worsening economic situation and the deterioration in the living conditions of the people, another factor that made the production and export of Commandaria more difficult was taxation.

Taxation was threefold: 10% on the value of the grapes (tithe), 10% on the value of the wine and 8% on exports.[44] In reality, taxation was much higher, for the producers were exposed to the machinations of the Ottoman tax officers and their local representatives who claimed for themselves a much bigger share. The Englishman Fairfield (1883) estimated the cumulative level of taxation at the end of the Turkish rule to have exceeded 37%. More details were provided by George Hill in his *History of Cyprus* cited before.

Psaras[45] considers that the unbearable taxation imposed by the Turks reduced the production and export of Commandaria drastically but also had the advantage that production was restricted to areas more suitable for this purpose that continued to produce wine according to the methods and standards applied

---

[43] Lusignano di Cipro, Stefano, ob. cit., 1973, p. 19.

[44] George Hill I, *History of Cyprus*, Vol. 4, Cambridge, 1908, p. 244.

[45] P. Psaras, *Commandaria The Apostle of Wines*, in Vines and Wines of Cyprus, 4000 Years of Tradition, Limassol, 1993, p. 91-106.

during the medieval golden age. The producer, he says, could not dispatch his wine before securing an official permission for the quantity he wanted to transfer to Limassol. This required prior inspection in the village. Arriving in Limassol, the owner had to present himself to the official weighbridge, where the wine was checked again and, in case there was a discrepancy with the quantity mentioned in the license, the seller paid heavy penalties.

The wine producer also had to comply with strict rules related to quality. Jovanni Mariti described the way the transactions were made: *"The deals are closed in the villages, so much for a load, and each load comprises 16 kouza. For the transport to the city, the wine must be placed in leather bags (askia) containing dregs. And, provided it stays in these bags for at least a year, its quality improves. The leather bags can be full or only partly filled and the wine does not suffer as long as there is a space on top. The farmer who sells the wine is responsible that it keeps its quality until the 15th of August the next year, no matter whether it has spent the year in his own or in the buyer's cellar. On that day it is inspected and if it has suffered, the seller must take it back. Otherwise, he has a right to be paid because the wine is not subject to alteration after the first year."*

CHAPTER VIII

THE TECHNOLOGY OF COMMANDARIA PRODUCTION

Pressing the grapes to yield the precious juice required for Commandaria production

Pressing the grapes to produce Commandaria requires high pressure because the grapes are first laid out in the sun to lose water and they are semi-dry when they reach the point of crushing. In Cyprus, this was done traditionally in special rooms called "linos" that housed various types of wooden presses and several pithars to store the grape juice for vinification. The name "linos" comes from the ancient Greek word "ληνός" which denotes "trough", an approximation for the flat-bottomed pit where the grapes were put to be crushed.

In its most advanced form, the wooden press of a "linos" employed two heavy-duty horizontal bars or beams (squared tree logs) bound to each other, that functioned as a second-degree lever. The two beams were placed one above the other for added weight. Each one measured 40 by 40 cm or more and the upper one, which was longer, reached up to 11 meters. On the backside of the room, the beams entered a recess or hole built into the stonemasonry of a strong thick wall that functioned as a fulcrum by preventing them from going up when the other end was pulled down. The system functioned like a nutcracker.

A wooden screw penetrating a helical socket at the far end of the upper beam caused the lever to move up and down, depending on the direction of the spinning. The base of the screw was fixed on a cylindrical boulder to multiply the force exerted on the beam when penetrated by the screw.

Turning the screw was done by two or more men pushing around a horizontal rod piercing the lower part of the screw.

The grapes to be pressed were placed under the far end of the lever in a flat-bottomed pit and were covered by a wooden board on which several logs were criss-crossed to take the pressure of the lever and spread it on a greater surface.

Employing a lever to construct a strong press, including the use of a "κοχλίας" (screw) or other equivalent method, was known from ancient times and was used in various situations, notably for the extraction of olive oil.

The oldest known facility for pressing grapes to produce wine in Cyprus dates from the late copper period and was brought to light during archaeological excavations at Alassa-Palaeotaverna at the lower end of the Kouris valley. The remains at this location also provided evidence for the use of a lever with associated weights to generate more pressure.[46] Lever presses with "κοχλίας" and weights existed in antiquity, both in Cyprus and elsewhere, and were more widespread during the Late Roman and Early Byzantine period (7th to 9th century). They were, however, smaller and were mainly employed to extract oil. Using a screw represented a significant

---

[46] Hadjisavvas, *Wine for the elite, olive oil for the masses: Some aspects of early agricultural technology in Cyprus*, In David J. Schloen (ed.), *Exploring the Longue Durée, Essays in Honor of Lawrence E. Stager*, Winona Lake, Indiana, Eisenbrauns, 2009, pp. 141-144.

technological advance, since it allowed to generate greater pressure and a better crushing.⁴⁷

Unfortunately, there is no written or other direct evidence about the use of the "lever-with-screw-technology" for pressing grapes in Cyprus during the rest of the Byzantine centuries. Although there is extensive literature describing various types of "linos", all of it refers to the last three hundred years and is largely based on descriptions of the few surviving specimens that were restored and preserved by the Cyprus Department of Antiquities as monuments of pre-industrial technology. An excellent review and summary was given by Ephrosyni Rizopoulou-Egoumenidou in 1989⁴⁸ and, more recently, in an unpublished paper presented at the "Days of History and Culture, Silikou" in June 2018. Most of the information in this chapter, including the pictures, derive from her work.⁴⁹

Not all the buildings housing a "linos" could be dated with certainty. The oldest one carrying a date is the one in the village of Kapedes from the year 1733. A bigger "linos" in the village of Omodhos is generally thought to have been built in the 14th century.

Once more, it was Giovanni Mariti who left us a reliable

---

[47] Sophocles Hadjisavvas, *Olive oil production in ancient Cyprus*, Report of the Department of Antiquities, *Cyprus* 1988 (Part 2), pp. 111-120; Sophocles Hadjisavvas, *Report of the Department of Antiquities, Cyprus* 1990, pp. 181-185; Sophocles Hadjisavvas, *Olive Oil Processing in Cyprus: From the Bronze Age to the Byzantine Period*, Studies in Mediterranean Archaeology 99, Göteborg, Åström Editions, 1992, pp. 45-46.

[48] Ephrosyni Rizopoulou-Egoumenidou, (*Viticulture and the traditional linos of Cyprus*), (Technology) 3, 1989, pp. 20-22.

[49] Ephrosyni Rizopoulou-Egoumenidou, (*From the vine to the pithar: The traditional linos of Cyprus as witnesses of pre-industrial technology*), paper presented at "Days of Culture, Silikou", June 1918, 13p.

account on the functioning of "linos" in the 18th century.[50] He described a simple type of press with a lever fixed on both sides in a wall. The screw went first through a log functioning as additional weight and then penetrated a helical socket in the middle of the horizontal beam. The pressure was exerted on the grapes put in a wooden barrel placed below the screw.

A "simple" screw press with a barrel (from Egoumenidou, 2018)

Before being pressed in this way, the grapes had typically remained spread on the roof for many days to lose water. They were then carried by hand or with shovels to a pit in a corner of the "linos", called "patitiri", where they were trampled by two barefooted men and beaten with wooden chops to yield as much

---

[50] Ciovanni Mariti, *Wines of Cyprus, Vine Planting to Harvesting. Wine Making to Marketing*, translated by Gwyn Morris, Athens, A. Nicolas Books, 1984 (Orig. 1772), p. 48

of their juice as possible. Only then were they put in the barrel for final pressing.

A "patitiri" placed in the corner of a "linos" (from Egoumenidou, 2018)

A very detailed description of a more sophisticated and powerful "linos" was given by Doozan, a French Consul in Larnaca (1852-1856), in a report dated 18 November 1855 on the oenology of Cyprus. The report was translated and published by Neoklis Kyriazis in 1931.[51]

Doozan's account of the construction and operation of a heavy-duty wine press is similar to the one given by Rizopoulou-Egoumenidou in 2018 concerning the "Linos of Lania", the only "linos" fully preserved in its original state. Lania is a village in the Kouris valley. It is perhaps worth reproducing here the key elements of Egoumenidou's description with pictures and a design.

---

[51] Jules Doozan, cited by Neoclis G. Gyriazis, (*The wine production of Cyprus*), in Κυπριακά Χρονικά τ. Η΄, 1931, p. 283-309. Triantafyllidou-Baladié, Yolande, "*Viticulture et vins de Chypre au milieu du 19e siècle*", In (Cypriot Studies) Vol. ΞΔ΄-ΞΕ΄ (2000-2001), Nicosia, Society of Cypriot Studies, 2003, pp. 513-559.

"The only 'linos' in Cyprus, in which the large leverage mechanism for crushing the grapes is preserved to this day, is in the village of Lania. The mechanism is housed in a stone-built building of an irregular rectangular shape. On the narrow side, towards one street, is the entrance with a double-leaf wooden door. There is a second entrance on the long side of the building. A staircase has been added to this side, leading up to the flat roof (see floor plan below), on which the grapes intended for pressing were laid out in the sun.

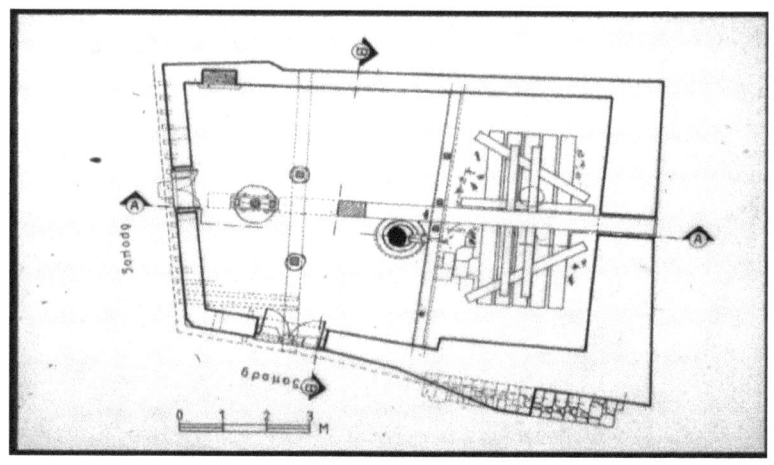

A floor plan of the Linos of Lania (from Egoumenidou, 2018)

The roof rests on two main transversal beams, each further supported in the middle by two wooden vertical posts or pillars. The distance between the posts differs so as to facilitate the operation of the press. The ones at the back of the room, where the grapes are crushed, are placed on either side of the longitudinal axis of the building and at a short distance from each other, because their role is (besides supporting the roof), to limit the movements of the long horizontal beam of the lever mechanism, which passes between them and enters a hole in the back wall. This wall is more than twice as thick as the other walls, a feature characteristic of buildings that house a linos. The other two pillars are spaced much further apart, leaving free space for the beams' movement inside them.

The 'mouklos' in the Linos of Lania and the way it was moved up and down by turning the screw around (from Egoumenidou, 2018)

An important element that serves the purpose of the press is the raised floor of the flat pit, laid with stone-slabs, where the grapes are placed for crushing. A horizontal transverse beam sitting on a low wall marks the border between the pit and the rest of the room. The pit is called tzyathin (from ancient Greek κύαθος=container or vessel). The mechanism for pressing the grapes comprises an elongated lever ('mouklos', from Greek μοχλός = lever) made of two beams (rectangular tree trunks), placed in such a way that one overlaps most of the other.

The two beams of the 'mouklos' are joined by wooden wedges piercing them vertically. The second beam increases the weight of the system. The 'mouklo's passes between the two posts at the back and enters the 'rhizomouklia', a deep rectangular recess or hole in the back wall of the winery. At the other end of the 'mouklos', inside a helical socket, rotates the 'adrachtin', a vertical wood screw, the base of which penetrates a cylindrical boulder. When the screw is turned around by the force of two or more men pushing the wooden arms or 'turners', it meanders inside the helical slot of the 'mouklos', causing the beam to be lowered or raised, depending on the direction of the rotation.

The entire system operates as a lever of the second degree, like a nutcracker. The force is exerted at the end of the beam by the penetrating screw and the weight of the boulder attached to it. The grapes placed in the pit below the beam are the resistance to the pressure, while the end of the beam inside the back-wall acts as a fulcrum. In Lania, the grapes intended for pressing were spread out, many days before, on the roof of the 'linos' to lose water in the sun. Then they were thrown down through a hole in the building's roof and spread out in the pit. The grapes were then covered with boards and crisscrossed logs under the raised mouklos, ready to be crushed. By pulling the other end of the mouklos down, the grapes in the pit were pressed down and crushed. The juice passed through an opening at the bottom of the pit, flowing into a pithar half-sunk in the lower floor of the linos. From there, the must was transferred to other pithars inside and outside the 'linos' to undergo vinification."

Covering the grapes with a wooden board and logs pushed under the mouklos to spread the pressure on a bigger surface (from Egoumenidou, 2018)

Archeological evidence about the use of the linos-technology during the Frankish period

Five and a half centuries after the Ottomans conquered Cyprus in 1571, there are hardly any remains of the agricultural buildings, machinery, and equipment used specifically during the Frankish period. The few purely Frankish villages, such as Syrka, were deserted and their remains gradually disappeared. In other villages, the buildings were put to other uses or were adjusted to the much smaller size of farms and ownerships prevailing in subsequent centuries.

Still, as mentioned earlier, one of the two "linos" in the village of Omodhos is considered to have been in operation during the Frankish period and this is mentioned in the declaration of this building as an "ancient monument" by the Cyprus Department of Antiquities. Rhizopoulou-Egoumenidou

(2018) speculates that this assessment was probably based on the presence of a Gothic-style doorway with associated pilasters on one of the building's walls, including a motive of continuous "canine-tooth" along the doorway's pointed arch (see picture below). She accepts these elements as indicative of the architectural styles introduced to Cyprus from the Latin crusader lands in Syria and Palestine but argues that they continued to be popular in Cyprus in later times too; she mentions several examples of such use, including a similar door at the northern entrance of the monastery of the Holy Cross in Omodhos, which bears a founding inscription dated 1816.

The doorway of the 'Omodhos linos' (from Egoumenidou, 2018)

Circumstantial evidence pointing to wide use of the heavy-duty linos-technology during the Frankish period

Archaeologists and academics may have their strict rules about what they can accept as evidence and what they consider mere speculation; but the absence of clear-cut proof should not be misunderstood as evidence that something didn't exist or didn't happen. Especially when there is plenty of circumstantial evidence pointing in the opposite direction.

The remains of the Frankish sugar mill of Colos and of the aqueduct carrying the water to rotate the milling stones of this facility are still standing today in their original position for everybody to see. Imagine, however, they had disappeared in the centuries that passed since they were built. Would anybody contest the existence of sugar mill technology in Frankish Cyprus when we have so much information about the production and export of sugar and molasses during this period?

Let us now apply the same principle to Commandaria. In previous chapters, we saw that the quantities of Commandaria produced during the Frankish period, notably during the 14th century, were exceedingly large. The feudal estates were operated and controlled by local "capitanos" and "apautors" who, as we saw for Silikou and Kilani, were people with deep roots in the area and quite experienced in winemaking. Considering, in addition, that the crushing and pressing of semi-dry grapes requires a lot of power, we are inevitably led to the conclusion that the heavy-duty grape presses we have described before must have been in wide use already at that time. For the royal estates of Kilani and Silikou, for the Grand Commandery of Colos and for the other large feudal estates, the motivation to find a way to crush thousands of tons of grapes within a short ripening period was obviously very strong.

There is plenty of other circumstantial evidence pointing in the same direction. The technology was not invented during the Ottoman period; it was known long before that as we have described earlier. We know, for example, that grape presses employing a lever with a screw and associated weights were already in use in France, the "mother country" of the Frankish feudal lords of Cyprus, during the 12th and 13th centuries. Bernard Lauvergeon studied the development of French pre-industrial presses and found that several types of wooden presses with a central screw and lever were in use in Burgundy very early.[52] Initially, the wooden screw was fixed on stakes sunk deep into the ground or was fixed with side timbers in underground pits to withstand the pressure (so-called *pressoirs à taissons*). In one case, in the *Clos de Chenôve* in the eastern part of Burgundy, a press made of oak wood was dated by means of dendrochronology to have been in place in 1238. It was refurbished in 1401, one year after the winery was reconstructed, then restored again in 1449.

The cost of such a heavy grape-press was not affordable to all. Only the big domains and the chateaux practicing monoculture could afford the cost of maintaining a heavy *pressoir* of this type. Sometimes they were owned by communities.

From the 15th century onwards or even before, there were also models in operation where the counterweight was provided by heavy boulders like those we have seen in the case of the Cypriot models (so-called *pressoirs à levier à contrepoids mobile*). Lauvergeon states that these were more prevalent in

---

[52] Bernard Lauvergeon, *Les grands pressoirs bourguignons, pré-industriels: essai de chronotypologie*, InSitu 5, 2004, Le patrimoine rural (1ère partie), pp. 1-35

Lorraine and Alsace and in neighbouring German territories. He estimates that this more advanced type of press was a development of the older models *à taissons*. Turning the screw was done by hand with the help of a simple horizontal lever but, in later models, a horizontal wheel was added to facilitate the participation of more people in this hard work.

A design of two *jumelle pressoirs* from Lauvergneon's study is shown below. He explains that the boulders at the base of the screw, weighing up to five and a half tons, were certainly in use in the mid-15th century, but were an adaptation of previous models. By rising in the air when the pressure became excessive, the boulders served both to increase the pressure and to control the operation of the press.

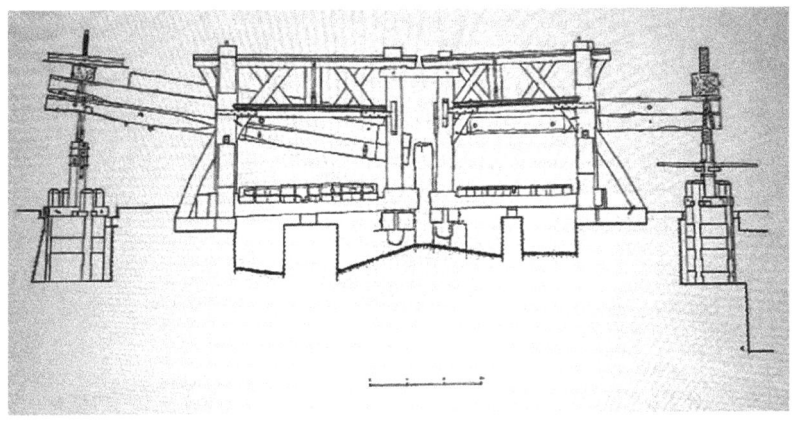

Lever presses with a moving counterweight at Chenôve, Côte-d'Or. (Relevé V. Lepais © Inventaire général, ADAGP, 1999 47). From B. Lauvergeon, ob. cit., 2004.

There are obvious similarities between the machines presented by Lauvergeon and the Cypriot model in the "Linos of

Lania". They are not exhausted in the use of boulders, and they didn't escape the attention of the French Consul Doozan cited before. In his 1855 report on the oenology of Cyprus, he states that *"the method of producing the liqueur wine in Cyprus is like that used in Burgundy for white wines. After exposure on the roof for 20 days, the grapes of choice are brought in baskets to the 'linos', which only the wealthiest vine growers have."*

In France or in Cyprus, putting in place such a costly machine was out of the reach of small farmers. Only the wealthier ones -and feudal lords before- could afford it. Neither was it possible to develope these advanced models overnight. As Bernard Lauvergeon informs us, the initial models in France required hard work by many people and needed frequent repairs so that *"the carpenters of the time were constantly on their feet"*.

It would not, therefore, be convincing to argue that the advanced linos-technology of the 18th and 19th centuries present in the villages of Cyprus was introduced and matured during the impoverished Ottoman centuries, when Commandaria production in Cyprus had lost much of its medieval glory. In the absence of a prototype, such an impressive apparatus would have required advanced engineering skills that were certainly lacking in the backward rural society of Cyprus under Turkish rule. The simple "linos" from the 18th century described by Mariti was not a prototype but, rather, an adaptation to the needs of smaller farms after the disappearance of the large feudal estates.

If the Burgundian model of a press with boulders was already in use in France in the 14th and 15th centuries, there is no reason to believe that this was not the case in Frankish Cyprus which, from a Commandaria production point of view, was living its golden age. Both the royal family and many of the nobles and feudal lords of Cyprus were of French origin and, although they came to Cyprus from the Holy Land, they had never broken their ties and contacts with the Latin West.

This does not mean that the technology could not have been developed concurrently and independently in each of the two countries. In the Mediterranean and Middle East region, it was used since ancient times for extracting oil from olives previously crushed with rolling boulders in special stone cavities.[53] Neither is it to be excluded that, in Cyprus, the technique had been adapted to the needs of wine production before the Franks arrived here at the end of the 12th century. Whatever the case, if we view medieval Cyprus as an "outre-mer" Frankish dominion and Burgundy as a metropolitan one, then the issue who benefitted first from the other's knowledge boils down to a chicken and egg question. There is nothing to gain from pursuing this matter further.

In search of the remains of medieval "linos"

We have argued earlier that the lack of findings concerning the location of medieval linos facilities (with the exception perhaps of the one in Omodhos), could be explained by assuming that the buildings were put to other uses during the 500 years that followed or were adjusted to the much smaller size of farms that prevailed during the Ottoman centuries. In other cases, the villages may have been deserted after the Ottoman conquest and their remains gradually disappeared.[54]

Silikou and Syrka (Siria) are good examples of these two categories. Silikou survived and became a purely Christian-Orthodox

---

[53] Sophocles Hadjisavvas, ob. cit., 1988, 1990, 1992
[54] Gilles Grivaud, *Villages désertés à Chypre*, Nicosia, 2009, pp. 73-78

community before it was turned again into a mixed Greek-Turkish Cypriot village. Syrka did not and is known today as an agricultural locality with a few old ruins. Given the Frankish past of both villages and the medieval glory of Silikou as a major royal estate producing large quantities of Commandaria, this pair is a prime candidate for a case study about what might have happened to the medieval linos facilities.

Silikou is known to have possessed several "linos" in the past. None of them survived intact to the present day, but their locations are known to the village elders. In the western part of the village, which is built on a slope levelling out at the top, there are remains of a rectangular building, traditionally referred to as "linos". It is approximately of the same size as the "Linos of Lania" and, from a location point of view, it offers several advantages because the level of the ground behind it is 4-5 meters higher.

The village elders confirm that the ruins of this building and the name "linos" are ancient, so old that they never heard of the place having been in operation. Even the ownership of the property is disputed. Several families (including the one of the author's mother), claim to have inherited a share of it from their forefathers, but nobody bothered to take the matter further. It was, therefore, left untouched and survived unchanged to the present day.

Undoubtedly, this structure was once a "linos" but we have no clue whether it was already in operation during the Frankish period or not. One thing is certain. The back-wall of this building was there since time immemorial to hold and support the elevated ground behind it. This ground flattened out at the point and must have looked like an extension of the flat roof of the "linos" when it was intact.

In the types of "linos" we described earlier, including the one in Lania, the grapes were spread on the roof of the building to dry, and from there, they were thrown down into the crushing pit through an opening. The practice of spreading the grapes on the roof for 20 days was also described by the French Consul Doozan (ob. cit.), writing in 1855. This was not very practical for big estates having to deal with hundreds of tons of grapes. The space on the roof was limited and, in addition, carrying the grapes in baskets up a staircase required arduous work.

This facility offered a crucial advantage in this respect. Behind the building there were thousands of square meters of flatland to lay the grapes out in the sun to dry for as many days as it was actually required to reach the recommended sweetness. From there, it was easy to feed the press at a constant rate by throwing the finished grapes through an opening on the flat roof of the linos. The terrain was thus put to the service of increasing the efficiency of crushing and enabled this press to deal with much bigger quantities of grapes over the limited ripening period.

Turning now to Syrka, which seems to be a location of considerable importance for the history of Commandaria, it is perhaps important to summarize first the information suggesting that a prototype of a "linos" was in operation there in medieval times (see also Constantinou, 2016).

Syrka (medieval Siria) is quoted in the sources as having existed at least from 1365 to 1571. The built-up area of Syrka was not big, and it was well-defined. In the centre of the settlement, there stood a large, heavy-duty construction that was demolished by the Turks in 1571 or was left in disrepair and collapsed in the centuries that followed. A Chapel was built on its ruins at the end of the 19th century. The parts visible today comprise a huge solitary wall standing next to the Chapel, 4,2 m long, 2,5 m high and 1,5 m wide, showing an inclination of 15% on the outside. It looks like an external support pilaster of an enormous building but is too big even for that. There are also remains under the northern wall of the Chapel, including a collapsed arched window filled with stones and plaster fallen from above. It was 'incorporated' in the wall of the Chapel. The convex piece of another arch lies there below too.

The Chapel's northern wall, and the remains below it, sit on another much wider wall, which was exposed during excavations going deep into the ground. To the East there are remains demarcating the eastern end of the old building, which is thereby clearly sketched: it was a heavy construction, 12-13 m wide and about 15 m long.

The view that this robust old building was a church is not supported by the evidence. Syrka was not a full-grown village but an estate with large underground cellars. There was no need to construct a big church there. The religious needs of the few Latin inhabitants were met by the Latin prior of nearby Silikou and the parish church of St. George. In the whole Latin Diocese of Limassol there were only two more churches: in Limassol and in Alaminos. An early Christian church (or the ruins of it) may have existed in Syrka, but it was probably located beyond this building's northern wall or in a nearby plateau where remains of mosaic floors were found.

A comparison with other Frankish-time constructions supports the view that this building was rather a 'utilitarian' edifice. Located in the middle of extensive vineyards and surrounded by large wine cellars, what else could that building actually have been than a facility associated with winemaking? some sort of a prototype of the "linos" that were certainly in operation in Cyprus. This would also explain the existence of the huge wall on the south side having a thickness of 1,5 meters or more. As we saw before, it was a usual practice for the wall acting as fulcrum for the heavy-duty levers of a "linos", to be twice as thick as other walls. The pressure they had to withstand when the lever was pulled down on the other side was shown to exceed 15 tons. The floor of the Syrka building is likely to have been much below today's level. The 'fulcrum wall' was even thicker down there.

Let us now describe these findings in more detail with the aid of pictures taken by Constantinou (2016). The Chapel of the Virgin Mary of Syrka was built by a man called Hadji-Thrasyboulos at the end of the 19th century, presumably for religious reasons. On the north side, he used the precarious remains of a previous construction, whereas, on the south side, he refrained from using a sturdy old wall standing right there (see picture).

The wall of "Syrka" pictured en face (previous page) and from the side (above).

As mentioned earlier, this robust wall is 4,2 meters long and one and a half meters wide at its base. It rises to two and a half or more meters above today's ground. On the inside, it is vertical, and part of it has collapsed. At its highest point, to the left, a light inclination towards the inside is clearly visible, indicating that the wall may have been 'going over' into a convex roof. On the outside, it is inclined with a gradient of 15%, narrowing in thickness the higher it goes up. On both ends, the wall is 'finished' making it look like a solitary construction. On the eastern end, it seems to be 'sitting' on a lower 'base' that probably extended to the right under the church.

The remains under the Chapel's northern wall

As the pictures show, the Chapel's northern wall is 'sitting' on the collapsed remains of a previous wall. The remains include at least two arches or arched windows. One of them is 'well-defi ned' and was 'incorporated' in the new wall.*

The contours of the arch are clearly visible, and a piece of its upper part lies down below the debris leaving a small 'cave' under it, now partly fi lled with loose stones. This is a clear sign that the win-dow was opening to the outside and was not built-in. Obviously, the remains of stones and plaster now fi lling the 'window' have fallen there from the upper part of the previous wall or from the roof, pushing down the upper convex part of the arch that now lies down below them.

Along the Chapel's northern wall, we can see on the ground the foundations of a thick wall at least 100 cm wide. The Department of Antiquities started excavations some thirty years ago on the northern side of this wall, going down about a meter. The assumption was that this wall may have belonged to an ancient church from the Byzantine or early Christian period. This initial assessment was probably based on information that pieces of floor mosaics were spotted in the area. However, Constantinou (2016), who grew up in Silikou, confirmed from personal knowledge that the last of these mosaic remains were not found near today's church but in another plot one hundred meters away, that dominates the area to the south.

Detail of the lower part of the arched window. (Note the visible internal surface of the arch on the left and the small 'cave' under the collapsed convex piece below).

The foundations of a thick wall along the northern wall of the Chapel of the Virgin Mary

Without excluding that an older church may have existed on the northern side of today's chapel, there would still be a need to explain why a chapel of whatever age would need a wall 130-150 cm thick. It is much more logical to assume that these foundations belonged to the same structure as the robust southern wall, making up some sort of 'utilitarian' medieval buildings like those found in other places (for example, the sugar factory of Colos). A surviving piece of masonry at the eastern end of the foundations, standing vertically against the northern wall, offers support to this view. It extends to the outer finish of the foundations on the ground and, interestingly, it seems to be connected to the findings on the southern side of today's Chapel.

*A piece of old masonry standing against the
northern wall of the Chapel of Syrka.*

In fact, if one would draw a straight line from the eastern edge of the huge southern wall to the southeastern corner of the Chapel, and then crossings the Chapel to the northern side, one would arrive exactly at the eastern 'face' of the masonry shown in the picture above. This line probably marked the eastern end of the old building. Only the semi-cyclical eastern "Holy" of the Chapel built later extends beyond this line.

We thus arrive at the external contours of the rectangular structure that lies below the Chapel of the Virgin Mary of Syrka. It was measuring 12-13 by 15 meters in size and was bearing all the typical characteristics of a medieval 'utilitarian' building. Its roof was probably convex-shaped and was covered by a thick layer of plaster, pieces of which ended up under the northern wall of the Chapel. The side walls may have also been covered with plaster, as shown by the presence of such plaster on the outer surface of the huge wall to the south of the Chapel and on a piece of the collapsed second arch to the north.

There remains to answer three important and quite pertinent questions concerning the huge southern wall of Syrka. Why was it so strong and inclined as if to support externally a huge building? Why was it so wide when the external pilasters of even the biggest cathedral are narrower? If it was part of the southern external wall of the building, why was it only four meters long when the building must have been about 15 meters long?

All three questions find an answer if we assume that the 'utilitarian' building of Syrka was a medieval "linos". In that case, this solitary wall would have been constructed specifically to offer enough resistance to the heavy wooden lever, the *mouklos*, of a sturdy grape press that was nesting in a recess or a 'hole' at its base, probably below today's ground level, where the wall was even thicker. The excavations along the northern wall showed it to continue deep into the ground, suggesting that the floor of the building was far below today's ground level.

As we saw when describing the "Linos of Lania", it was an established practice to construct walls twice the normal thickness when they were used as a fulcrum for a sturdy lever press. The upward pressure exercised on the wall holding the arm of the lever when the other end was pulled down was enormous. It was big enough to keep a group of boulders chained together and weighing up to five tons being pulled up above the ground. Lauvergeon estimated the pressure exerted on the wall to be over 15 tons and that on the grapes 21 tons.

In Cyprus, the practice was to continue turning the screw until the boulders were raised 30 cm above the ground and to leave them hanging there for at least an hour. The grapes below gave up the last drop of juice. This also explains the many suspensions in the wine that gradually settled to the bottom, changing the colour of Commandaria from red to yellowish, as several medieval authors inform us.

In Syrka, the rest of the walling must have been less strong and did not survive to the present day. According to Gilles Grivaud (ob. cit.), Syrka was last mentioned in the sources in 1566. The Turks considered the Franks of Cyprus and the Latin Church as their archenemies and destroyed most of the buildings and churches directly belonging to them. It was at this time, for example, that they levelled to the ground the ten or more Christian Chapels of Silikou (Constantinou, 2016). They kept the sugar factory of Colos because they settled themselves in the area and sugar production was a lucrative business. In Syrka, however, there is no trace of Ottoman presence. To this day, there is not a single piece of land that belongs to Turkish Cypriots. The former village was left to decay. For a long time, stones from Syrka were carried away to serve in the construction of new dwellings in the neighbouring villages. It is not therefore surprising that after 550 years, only a very strong masonry like the one required to support a linos lever could survive.

There is no definite information as to the beginning of the operation of the "linos of Syrka", if that was in fact what existed there. Constantinou (2023) analysed the historical evidence and concluded that the "pithar of Syrka", unearthed in 1956, was probably constructed by John Lascaris during the reign of King Peter I. He put forward convincing evidence that Lascaris was strongly motivated to have the symbols of the papacy and of royal power engraved on his new pithars. And he was out to enrich himself quickly. Clearly, the time was ripe for the construction of a new "linos".

Lascaris was a Byzantine adventurer expelled from Constantinople, known to be quite eager to become rich one way or another. In 1365, he is reported to have been on the galley of King Peter I when he captured Alexandria. The attackers loaded about half of their 150 galleys with rich spoils and returned to Cyprus before the Mamluk enforcements arrived from Cairo. He continued to take part in similar raids.

Before coming to Cyprus, Lascaris had travelled extensively in Western Europe in the service of the popes of Avignon, presumably to help reunite the Churches. He is therefore likely to have encountered the technology used elsewhere to press the grapes for making liqueur wine. Clearly, he had the motivation, money and knowledge to proceed with the construction of a new "linos" in Syrka. Judging from the dimensions of the building we described before, it was providing enough space to house a heavy grape press like the ones described by Lauvergne being in operation in Burgundy in the 14th century and thereafter.

CHAPTER IX

COMMANDARIA IN MODERN TIMES

A medieval legacy to honour and to cherish

The legacy left for Cyprus by the wine production and trade activities of the Knights of St. John and the medieval kings of Cyprus continued to be cherished several centuries after their departure from the island. Over time, the name Commandaria became dominant and was used to describe the type of sweet wine produced in Cyprus since ancient times, irrespective of whether it was now produced in the villages of the former Commandery or St. John or in those that made up the fiefs controlled by the Crown.

Writing in 1772, Jovanni Mariti, who was a Correspondent Member of the Academy of Agricultural Experts of Florence, felt the need to inform his readers that the designation Commandaria was not referring only to wine produced in the former Grand Commandery of the Knights of St. John but also in other traditional areas.

Likewise, for historians like De Mas Latrie, the designation Commandaria was a cultural heritage bestowed upon the entire wine-growing region of Cyprus by the Frankish period and not something to be viewed in strict geographical terms., Writing in 1837, De Mas Latrie spoke about *"the types of wine produced in the southern slopes of the Mount Olympus, from Troodos until Maheras and the Mount of the Cross (Stavrovouni) to the East".*[55] In the same way, Constantius, Archbishop of Sinai, who visited Cyprus in 1776, spoke about Commandaria as *"originating in the areas of the island which are called Commandery, between the Mount Olympus and the towns of Limassol and Paphos where the seat and the tradition of the Commandery of the Order of the Templars and of the Knights of St. John were to be found."*[56]

The Commanderies of the Hospital were, of course, much smaller than the area implied by the descriptions of De Mas Latrie and Constantius, but this only serves to confirm that both of them were not so much interested in geographical accuracy. They just wanted to emphasize the legacy left by the medieval knights, as they saw it from their individual standpoint and convictions.

De Mas Latrie, being a child of post-Napoleonic France, saw the knights as old-time Frenchmen to whom the Cypriots were deeply indebted because the wine of Cyprus *"is in big demand thanks to the designation 'wine of the Commandery' left to them by our knights."*[57]

Constantius of Sinai, on the other hand, being a Greek Orthodox ecclesiastic, emphasized first of all the role of the religious Orders of the Temple and the Hospital, but placed the production of Commandaria in the frame of Greek traditions and classical archetypes as was the fashion during the period of

---

[55] *De Mas Latrie, ob. cit., 1837, p. 90*

[56] *Constantius, Archbishop of Sinai, (Description of the Famous Monastery of the Virgin Mary of Kykkos) with an Annex on "Κυπριάς Χαρίεσσα και Επίτομος", Venice, 1819, cited by Claude Delaval Cobham, Excerpta Cypria, Cambridge, 1908, p. 311.*

[57] *De Mas Latrie, ob. cit., 1837, p. 90.*

the Enlightenment. In his eyes, Commandaria was *"the fragrant nectar of Zeus which flows abundantly from the vineyards of his beloved son Bakhus."* And he continued by stating that *"this excellent wine is in great demand in Europe"*.[58]

Both historians agree that Commandaria continued to be in great demand in Europe at the beginning of the 19th century, and that is what really matters from the point of view of the history of Commandaria.

It was probably the fame and reputation of the wines of Cyprus that motivated Jules Doozan during his service as Consul of France in Larnaca (1852-1856) to report back home in great detail in 1855 about the methods of cultivation and the oenological practices applied in Cyprus. We have already mentioned his view that the grape presses used in Cyprus were like those in Burgundy.

It was in this same year that another Frenchman, Albert Gaudry, in his book *Recherches Scientifiques en Orient*, dedicated an extended chapter to the viticulture and oenology of Cyprus and concluded that *"Cypriot wines are justly counted among the best in the world"*.[59]

The decline in Commandaria production: the reasons

We have already discussed the deterioration of the living conditions of the people of Cyprus described by William Turner in

---

[58] *Constantius,* ob. cit.,1908, p. 311.
[59] Albert Gaudry, *Recherches Scientifiques en Orient, Entreprises par les Ordres du Gouvernement pendant les Années 1853-1854 et Publiées sous les Auspices du Ministère de l'Agriculture, du Commerce et des Travaux Publics*, Paris, Imprimerie Impériale, 1855.

1815 and the consequent reduction in the number of taxpayers in the early decades of the 19th century. However, according to the same author, the demand for Commandaria continued to be substantial and exports were now destined, besides Venice, to the Black Sea region. The construction of new "linos" wineries at about the same time, such as the one preserved to the present day in the village of Lania in the Kouris valley, testify to the continued importance of Commandaria production in traditional areas. The "linos" of Lania was constructed in 1822 by a certain Christophis Meramou. Linos facilities are known to have been in operation in the first half of the 19th century in several other places (Omodhos, Capedes, Kakopetria, Fikardou etc.). In a report describing the properties of the Holy Monastery of Kykkos prepared in 1879 at the request of the first British High Commissioner to Cyprus, there is mention of five "linos" wineries owned by the monastery at various places.[60] Other than Commandaria, only Muscat and Morocanella, two other liqueur wines produced in small quantities, required the use of a "linos" facility.

One of the main reasons for the decline of Commandaria production towards the end of the 19th century was the rise of other types of wine and the associated change in tastes and demand both in Cyprus and abroad. We have already referred to the figures published by Michael de Vézin in 1804, according to which the production of ordinary red wines in Cyprus exceeded that of Commandaria already during the second half of the 18th century (175 000 *kouza* versus 150 000 *kouza*, respectively). Jovanni Mariti informs us that ordinary wine was consumed

---

[60] Chysostomos, Abbot of Kykkos, (*The Holy, Royal and Stavropegiac Monastery of Kykkos)*, Cyprus, Holy Monastery of Kykkos, 1969, p. 108.

locally and on ships, in contrast to Commandaria that was exported to the West. William Turner, speaks of a much lower production of both Commandaria and table wine, adding that this inferior quality table wine was consumed locally and in Turkey.

A radical change in European vine growing occurred in the second part of the 19th century that brought Cyprus in the spotlight of developments but seems to have benefitted mainly the production of table wines. Starting in 1864, many vineyards in France and other European countries were destroyed by P*hylloxera*, an insect that attacks the roots of vines of European cultivars of *vinis vinifera*. Fortunately, Cyprus remained free of this pest, the only place in Europe to do so. Although scientists later discovered that American rootstocks were more resistant to phylloxera and replaced the damaged vineyards, until this happened wine production dropped drastically to the benefit of places like Cyprus. Several western countries tried to use grafts from Cyprus and, in this way, genetic material from the island found its way to France, Spain, and other places, providing 'ancestral' material for the famous varieties prevailing there to this day. In historical terms, this seems to have been the second time that Europe benefitted from Cypriot know-how in wine production. Already during the Middle Ages, the Knights of St. John, who owned estates in many European countries, took advantage of the knowledge they gained in Cyprus in producing Commandaria to improve the quality of liqueur wines in other places too. Some people believe that it is in this way that liqueur wines such as Madeira, Marsala and Tokai received their first boost.

In Cyprus itself, Commandaria does not seem to have benefitted much from the upheavals caused by the phylloxera epidemic. After the establishment of British rule in 1878, the administration promoted the production of industrial materials of agricultural origin, including wine and alcohol. Viticulture expanded and, over the next 30-40 years, the inhabitants of the mountainous and semi-mountainous areas of the island engaged in an arduous process to till the slopes of many a hill, using primitive hand tools. Wine production increased, but to the detriment of quality. The example of the pioneer Hadjipavlou family from Silikou, who had established an industrial-type winery in Limassol in 1844, was followed by other companies in the early 20th century. Soon, most of the grapes found their way to the industrial wineries of Limassol, which specialized in the production of table wines for domestic consumption and export, and produced several other alcoholic products (pure alcohol, brandy, *eau de vie de vin*, ouzo etc.). In the villages, a sizable share of grapes was turned into raisins and to a low-quality red wine for personal and local use. Zivania, a type of grappa, was also produced locally from the wine lees, using simple branding facilities.

These changes occurred to the detriment of Commandaria, the production of which went down sharply. Owning a "linos" has always been a costly affair and its operation was an arduous process. The traditional system of production could not persist under the new conditions and the "linos" wineries gradually declined in importance. The last ones seem to have stopped functioning in the early decades of the 20th century.

Systematic revival and upgrading after 1950

Immediately after World War II, the British administration of Cyprus introduced measures to protect and upgrade viticulture and winemaking. A "Law for the Protection of Wine Designations" was passed in 1950, allowing the adoption of regulations concerning the production and designation of wines. However, no such regulations were adopted until Cyprus became independent in 1960.

Soon after, the Department of Cooperative Development of the new Republic put forward and implemented plans for the creation of cooperative local wineries in all major Commandaria producing villages using traditional methods and standards. Once established, these local wineries signed long-term contracts with the major wine making companies in Limassol which undertook to purchase all quantities produced, and to market them under their own labels after appropriate storage and aging. Next to the knowledge and expertise that had come down from generation to generation, wine experts employed by the Limassol wineries provided further advice and controlled the quality of the final product.

In 1973, the first regulations for the control of the origin and designation of Cypriot wines entered force under Law 59/73. A "Committee of Wine Experts" was set up to control the oenological practices and organoleptic and other characteristics of protected designations of origin in order to ensure their authenticity and quality. Under these regulations, the Council of Ministers issued in 1990 decree K.D.P. 41/90, defining the specifications and geographical delimitation for producing wine eligible to be denominated Commandaria.

The "Commandaria area", as it came to be called, comprises only fourteen villages (Silikou, Agios Georgios, Monagri, Doros, Lania, Agios Mamas, Kapilio, Zoopigi, Kalo Chorio, Agios Konstantinos, Agios Pavlos, Louvaras, Gerasa and Apsiou) all of them in the District of Limassol. These vilages were popularly known as "Koumandarochorka", the "villages of Commandaria", for quite a long time and had never ceased to produce this type of wine using the old methods and specifications. They represent the core of the area used to produce Commandaria during the Middle Ages by the Knights of St. John (the seven eastern ones) and by the royal domains and fiefs belonging to noble families of Cyprus (the seven western ones). Their selection was based on this tradition but also because they were deemed to be endowed with the most favourable conditions to produce quality Commandaria (altitude, soil, yield per hectare and the prevalence of the local varieties Mavro and Xynistery, which are the only ones allowed).

Regrettably, the Commandaria area could not avoid falling victim to the massive relocation of rural people towards the cities that characterized the first decades after Cyprus' independence. Most of the villages in the vine growing area of southern Cyprus lost a major share of their inhabitants, especially younger ones, who moved to Limassol to attend schools and to search for more remunerative occupations. As a result, most of the cooperative local wineries established in the 1960's ceased operation relatively early, but some of them were taken over by private entrepreneurs who continued the tradition.

In more recent decades, several new privately-owned wineries were established in the Commandaria region benefitting from the additional incentives provided under European law to produce quality products and wines with a protected designation of origin and/or geographical indication.

It is worth summarizing the major factors that have contributed to this revival, which continues unhalted to the present day. Of course, nothing of this would have been possible without the persistent efforts of the people in the countryside who kept the traditions alive and continued to produce Commandaria even during difficult times. Commandaria is part and parcel of the history and rural culture of Cyprus since ancient times and probably the most ancient wine denomination in the world. Preserving this tradition has a value that can hardly be measured in monetary terms.

A strong impetus for the revival of Commandaria production and for the improvement of the quality of all Cypriot wines was provided by the failure –and forceful final abandonment upon accession of Cyprus to the European Union in 2004- of the counter-productive set of policies implemented during decades by successive Cypriot governments in the vines and wines sector. Centred on the guaranteed purchase and disposal of all quantities of grapes produced in the villages, this system amounted to a managed gradual abandonment of vine growing that could hardly find outlets for a set of products no longer sought by the markets abroad. In effect, the system favoured the subsidized production of low-quality table wines and alcohol by the major "industrial" wineries of Limassol and Paphos for the sake of helping to address a perceived problem of massive surpluses.

It was fortunate that, in the margins of this mainstream support system, the government started early providing technical assistance and financial support for setting up local wineries to produce wines of distinct character and better quality.

The focus on Commandaria was natural, given its long tradition. It was also favoured by the increase in demand, mainly by tourists who, following the general trend to prefer "produits du terroir", purchase this exceptional product, which they identify with the history and culture of the island of Cyprus. During the preparations for accession to the European Union, the long-standing EU policies on protected designations of origin and geographical indications further injected and speeded-up local efforts for the characterization and geographical specification of Cypriot agricultural products, Commandaria being first and foremost among them.

The Cyprus Department of Agriculture (of which the author of this book was Director from 1996 to 2005) took up the challenge and implemented several decisive steps to put the production of Commandaria on a fresh path. First, during the negotiations for accession to the European Union, it was ensured that the national protected designation of origin "Commandaria" was accepted by the EU and was entered in the list of protected designations along with other famous European wines. Vine growers and rural entrepreneurs received additional support to restructure their plantations, set-up new wineries and modernize existing ones.

More than anything, Commandaria received a strong boost by three types of support provided under Cyprus's first Rural Development Programme prepared by the Department of Agriculture and part-financed by the EU. Under the first one, vine growers were paid a set sum to cover the additional cost involved in meeting the specifications of quality products such as Commandaria. Under the second one, a similar amount was paid out to compensate farmers for continuing to practice agriculture in mountainous and disadvantaged regions, such as the area designated for the production of Commandaria. Finally, vine growers could take part in a so-called agri-environmental scheme and refrain from using herbicides in the catchment areas of rivers and streams that often ended up in the island's water supply system.

The liberalized EU internal market and the free circulation of goods after accession to the EU rewarded these efforts by increasing demand and prices, making Commandaria production (and the cultivation of vines of the specified varieties) much more remunerative. It is only hoped that this trend will continue in the years to come, giving back to Commandaria the place it deserves in the international market based on its distinct qualities and glorious past.

Continuing an age-long tradition, the residents of the designated rural communities and their elected representatives undertook to promote their product with fervor and zeal, having realized that Commandaria is a valuable asset and a legacy, the economic and cultural importance of which is not only of short-term nature. The Commandaria museums created in various communities and the festivals organized alternately by the communities of the region testify that this wine is part and parcel of Cyprus' rural culture and traditions and has been so from time immemorial.

As a full member of the European Union after 2004, Cyprus adopted the package of policies applying to the wine sector all over Europe, including market support, promotion and marketing support, direct payments and payments for the provision of environmental, climate and biodiversity services. Last but not least, the full EU package on quality policies and protected designations of origin was applied in Cyprus too.

Like other vine-growing countries, Cyprus was subject to the system of planting rights which provided for a short time horizon of four years for replanting any vineyards grubbed up or abandoned, otherwise they were lost. The long-lasting downward trend in the island's total area planted with vines had consequently led to a massive shrinkage of Cyprus' national reserve of planting rights. This, in effect, would have made any future recovery by improving the quality of domestic wines impossible.

Although the system was to run out in the second decade of the twenty first century, the EU set up a high-level group in 2012 to examine a possible extension. Its work culminated in a recommendation to prolong the system for, possibly, many more years. Fortunately, a provision was introduced which allowed small countries to opt out. Cyprus did so in 2014.

More than anything, Cyprus made use of the EU rules concerning Protected Designations of Origin and Geographical Indications. Three types of quality designations were adopted in accordance with the relevant EU regulation: protected designations of origin (PDOs), geographical indications (Limassol, Paphos, Larnaca and Nicosia), and wines of a specific variety designation (e.g., Maratheftico). It goes without saying that Commandaria was the first wine to be reconfirmed as a PDO under this legislation. In the meantime, more Cypriot wines received the PDO label (e.g., Laona-Akamas and Pitsilia).

The obstacles for the recovery of Commandaria production have now been removed and its future looks brighter. For a wine that justifiably claims to be Europe's first designation of origin, receiving a PDO label looks like a modest recognition of its remarkable pathway through history. In the modern world of free competition among thousands of quality wines, Commandaria must find its place on the shelves of shops and supermarkets. Buyers should be aware that this is not just another alcoholic drink. It is rather a living monument of wine making and drinking from Homeric times to the present day.

END

www.ingramcontent.com/pod-product-compliance
Ingram Content Group UK Ltd.
Pitfield, Milton Keynes, MK11 3LW, UK
UKHW020244240426
12048UKWH00026B/1598